BE MY
FRIEND

BE MY FRIEND

THE ART OF GOOD RELATIONSHIPS

PATRICIA STERNBERG

bridgebooks

THE WESTMINSTER PRESS
Philadelphia

Book Design by Alice Derr

First edition

bridgebooks
Published by The Westminster Press®
Philadelphia, Pennsylvania

PRINTED IN THE UNITED STATES OF AMERICA
9 8 7 6 5 4 3 2 1

Library of Congress Cataloging in Publication Data

Sternberg, Patrica.
  Be my friend.

  "Bridgebooks."
  1. Interpersonal relations. 2. Friendship.
I. Title.
HM132.S7 1983   302   83-10254
ISBN 0-664-26007-1 (pbk.)

To my foundations in friendship, then and now

Betsy Bowman   Dolly Beechman

Patsy Bergstrom   Anne Strathman

Contents

Acknowledgments

I am indebted to every friend I've ever had and everyone whose friend I've ever been.

Special thanks are due to Dr. Geraldine DePaula for getting the whole project started and sharing her good advice along the way; to Richard, David, Ruth, and Anne Sternberg without whose assistance in a hundred ways this book would not have been written; and to Dolly Beechman for her invaluable assistance.

I would like to thank the following people for sharing with me their personal opinions and feelings on friendship:

Terry Bagley
Pat Bennett
Carolyn Black
Elizabeth Bowman
Ian Calderon
Sandy Carl
Connie Clark
Marie Clark
Seena Corbman
Richard Cutler
Mira Felner
Janet Goodrich
Laura Hobe
Kathy Jedrziewski
William Johnson
Dennis Jones
Kay King

Dan Koetting
Gloria Hayes Kremer
Georgia Lehman
Harry Lines
Marjorie W. Longley
Rosalie Lush
James Manos
Monica May
Nancy Minnich
Dr. Abram Plon &
   Associates
Vera Roberts
Michael Rutenberg
Dr. Nathan Schnall
Marvin Seiger
Jack J. Sternberg
Anne Strathman
Eugene Strathman
Julie Thompson
Rosilyn Wilder
Edwin Wilson
Dorothy Woolfolk

And special thanks to the dozens of my students at Hunter College who participated in my survey on friendship.

Introduction

Friendship is as difficult to define as that other illusive term—LOVE. In fact, many of the same elements are found in both relationships.

There are as many different definitions of the word *friend* as there are people who have a friend or who are a friend. Yet, with definitions certain words recur over and over again; loyalty, trustworthiness, acceptance, and understanding are the most popular.

The phrase heard most often to describe a friend is, "Someone who's there when I need him."

Friendship has been important to me as long as I can remember. I have one friend I haven't seen in ages, yet we're still in touch after forty-five years.

I am a person who reaches out for friendship, and I will bend over backwards, if need be, to make a friendship work. But I know that kind of outgoing behavior isn't possible for everyone. Some people must wait until friendship is offered.

Friendship is a theme that I have explored in a variety of ways over the years. It has been a theme in several of my children's plays—for example, *Daddy Was a Leprechaun.* In that play one of the characters says: " 'Friend,' that's a funny word. What does it mean anyway?"

That's a song cue, of course, and the lyric begins, "A friend is someone you like, someone who likes you." So here I am many years later still exploring the same theme.

The idea of doing a book on friendship really started the year I worked in a mental hospital as a drama therapist. There, the value of friendship, or more specifically the lack of it, was dramatically illustrated.

Relationships were quickly formed on the basis of physical attraction, but mutual respect was sadly lacking.

One evening when I was working with a group of women, we began to discuss friendship. We talked about the qualities we looked for, and the qualities we brought to a relationship. We talked about what friendship meant to us in our lives. Most of the women knew what they wanted or thought they wanted, but few had little idea of what they could offer.

Another fact that came out most vividly was that the lack of friends and friendship had been a contributing factor in many of the participants' mental illness. "There was nobody I could talk to" was the common complaint.

Another factor that contributed heavily to this feeling of loneliness was the lack of inner resources. Many of these women stayed in severely destructive relationships just to have somebody—anybody. They had not learned to be with themselves, let alone enjoy their own company. Many of them stayed in abusive marriages or all-devouring family situations. The sense of self-worth in the hospital population of both men and women was unbelievably low.

Our explorations on friendship became the highlight for many of the women who had never talked to others about similar feelings.

Many of the questions, thoughts, and emotions that came out of those discussions have stayed with me. Anyone who has ever worked with this population knows that their concerns are similar to those of the rest of us so-called "normal" people, but their concerns are magnified.

Additionally, as a teacher in a large college in a metropolitan area, I see daily how the friendship routines work or don't work. I see a student devastated because a best friend failed to fulfill a promise, or another person elated because a friend remembered her birthday with a special celebration. I see the drama of friendship at work every day.

However, the most important reason for writing this book is a personal one to say THANK YOU. Thank you to all the wonderful, beautiful, glorious people in my life I have been privileged to call FRIEND.

CHAPTER 1

What Is a Friend?

"Why is it," an actress from Pennsylvania says, "that it's so hard for some friends to share the really good times? There's always someone who will give me a hand when I'm broke or between jobs. It's easy for people to sympathize with you when you're the one who's down-and-out. But what about the good times? I need someone to share those too."

She continues: "A friend to me is someone who can also enjoy your success. When you're on the rise and she's not, it still doesn't matter. That friend is just as happy for your success as she would be for her own. You are both confident about your friendship.

"One friend of mine always helps me out when I'm in trouble, but where is he when things are really great for me? Everyone talks about a 'fair-weather friend.' Well, this person is more like a 'foul-weather friend.' He's only around when trouble strikes. I can't figure it out. Maybe it's because he doesn't see our relationship as equal. He always has to be the benevolent partner."

Cicero defines friendship as "a complete accord on all subjects human and divine, joined with mutual goodwill and affection." He goes on to advise, "All I can do is urge on you to regard friendship as the greatest thing in the world; for there is nothing which so fits in with our nature or is so exactly what we want in prosperity or adversity."

"Complete accord on all subjects" may be too much to ask of any person, but no one will dispute "mutual goodwill and affection" are devoutly to be wished.

"Prosperity *or* adversity"—it's interesting that Cicero would balance the two as equally important. A friend is someone who's there when you need him, someone who will share both your sorrow and your joy.

An old Roman definition of friendship is *participes curarium*, which means "partners in care."

That sounds very much like a young advertising executive who defines a friend: "Someone who shares and cares . . . and the person can be a man or a woman."

Dictionary definitions of the word *friend* include: "A person whom one knows well and is fond of; an intimate associate; a close acquaintance; a person attached to another by feelings of affection or personal regard."

A thirty-eight-year-old second-grade teacher puts it simply. She says, "A friend is somebody you like and who likes you."

Benjamin Franklin said, "A father's a treasure; a brother's a comfort; a friend is both."

William Penn wrote, "A true friend unbosoms freely, advises justly, assists readily, adventures boldly, takes all patiently, defends courageously and continues a friend unchangeably."

That's a pretty tall order in today's world, but William Penn was known as a good and just man, who gave as much of himself to others as he expected in return.

MORE DEFINITIONS

In a recent survey among college men and women, *friend* was defined this way:

> "A friend is someone I trust. There are different levels of trust; therefore, different levels of friends."
> "Somebody I can count on when it counts."
> "A friend is somebody you can sit in the same room with and not have to talk to."
> "Somebody I care about, trust, and love."
> "Someone who enjoys me for what I am, not for what he'd like me to be."
> "A friend is the one who leaves the last piece of cake for you when she really wants it."

As you can see, friendship is a very personal thing and has many definitions. Everyone has different kinds of friends in life.

Children begin friendships very simply with those who are near by—who come out to play. They interact with each other and the environment. Sometimes the activity involves a give-and-take be-

14

tween them. Other times they do similar tasks together. But just being at the same place at the same time can provide the basis for a child's friendship.

When children go to school, their choices for friends widen. In high school during the teen years, there is a greater variety of interests and a greater mobility which make possible a wider selection of friends.

Friendship becomes all-important to adolescents. They see themselves through their friends. These relationships are often intense and central to good mental health. It is a time of exploration of the self and others, a time for testing loyalties and self-disclosure.

Those who go to college usually select friends with similar interests, whether in their field of study or in extracurricular activities. Those who train for a career come in contact with others who have similar interests and goals.

Many college friendships are built on a mutually expanding universe, learning things together. There is a special bonding that occurs during this particularly intense period of growth. It is a time for sharing dreams and ambitions, for testing one's ideas and philosophy on life.

Friendship, during this period, is often characterized by long and deep conversations probing the psyche and the universe and frequently lasting into the wee hours of morning or night.

Out in the marketplace or mainstream of life, one finds co-workers, others in a similar field, plus all the past friends and associations. Frequently, co-workers have only their work in common. Theirs is an acquaintanceship that does not cross the bridge to friendship.

When people get older, however, and busier with work and family, or with both, often there is little time to cultivate new friends. The cycle repeats itself, and once again proximity becomes the primary criterion for friendship.

Some people think if they just had a friend their whole life would be better. What they don't realize is that friendship doesn't just *happen*. Someone makes it happen. Learning to make friends is a skill like any other. Some people have a greater aptitude for it than others. Indeed, you might say there are those who have a real talent for making friends. Whether it's an aptitude or a talent, it takes skill, like learning to play golf. You may be able to hit the ball before you learn the game, but there are fine points like putting and chipping. Even the pros continue practicing their putting and trying to

15

improve their swing. Having a friend and being one takes practice too.

What does the word *friend* mean to you? What do you look for in a friendship? Or does friendship seem just to happen for you?

A drama teacher in Ohio says, "What I look for in a friend is someone who is considerate and honest and shares my interests . . . a person who's on the same wavelength." She paused thoughtfully for a moment and then added, "Oh, yes, any friend of mine has to like my dog too." She chuckled at her own realization. "That's important to me. It might sound silly, but I don't think I could have a really good friend who didn't like animals!"

"I think it's an emotional reaction," an author from New York says. "I can tell immediately if I'm attracted to a person or not." There is a certain openness about some people which appeals to me. When that's there, a little buzzer goes off in my head that says, 'That person could be my friend.' But finding a friend has to be a two-way street. The other person has to make some effort too."

A textile salesman says: "Seek and ye shall find does not apply to friendship. It is a 'result,' not an 'action.' "

YOUR BEST FRIEND

Stop and think for a moment about your friends. Who is—or was—your best friend? What are some of the qualities that attracted you to that person? Here are some answers to the last part of this question: "Who is your best friend, and why?"

A thirty-year-old secretary says: "My best friend is there when I need a friend. It's as simple as that."

A medical technician answers the question this way: "She's honest and easygoing, and likes to have a good time. She's been my best friend for twenty years and she's always there when I need her."

"My best friend is interested in me. Although we have mostly different interests, she cares about my interests too—just because that's a part of my life." This comes from a twenty-six year-old woman in Pennsylvania.

A middle-aged accountant thought for a moment and then admitted: "The best friend I ever had was back in high school. We had the same goals socially, athletically, and intellectually. He wasn't afraid to be critical. He could give you a pat on the back or a swift kick. Whatever his comments were, they were meaningful."

A housewife in New Jersey answers the question: "My best friend is fun to be with. She's an upbeat person and she's smart. She makes me think about a lot of different things. And she respects my opinions even when we disagree."

"My best friend always had faith in me, as I did in my friend. I love the *essence* of that person. We both have the ability to grow and change and accept each other's differences—and those times we couldn't accept the differences, we could laugh about it."

"She's never let me down," a thirty-eight year-old editor offers. "She's the first person I will go to in time of need. I trust her. She has a tremendous willingness to share my concerns."

WHO IS YOUR BEST FRIEND, AND WHY?

Answer the question for yourself. Who is your best friend, and why? What is it about the relationship that makes it special?

Ten responses heard frequently to the question "Why?" among both men and women from a variety of backgrounds are the following:

1. "He's loyal. He's there when I need him."
2. "We have common interests. We like the same things and enjoy doing things together."
3. "My friend is honest and accepting."
4. "She's fun to be with and easy to talk to."
5. "My friend is someone I can trust and share myself with."
6. "She's intelligent and has a good sense of humor."
7. "He's always on my side. He's supportive of me."
8. "We can talk about anything with no fear of judgment on either side."
9. "It's a feeling of mutual respect."
10. "She's adventurous. We discover new things together."

FAMOUS FRIENDSHIPS

There have been many famous friendships in history as well as in literature. George Washington and General Lafayette, Ernest Hemingway and F. Scott Fitzgerald, Maxwell Perkins and Thomas Wolfe.

Historically, only men's friendships were lauded as the one beautiful and true relationship. Women were thought incapable of such a lofty relationship among themselves. (Most of these opinions were voiced by men, however.) One of the most significant victories to come out of the women's movement in the 1970s was to open women's eyes to their own potential for many things, including friendship. It is no longer necessary for a woman to depend on a man to ensure a social life. Women can have women friends who are as important in their lives as men.

Women are learning what men have known for years. A friend helps a friend whenever, wherever he can: in the home, on the job, or in the marketplace. The Old Boys Network is a perfect example of this helping hand. The New Girls Network is on its way.

Shakespeare included the importance of friendship as a plot device in many of his plays. Sometimes those friendships caused conflicting loyalties such as in *Othello*. Othello chose to believe in the loyalty of his friend, Iago, rather than in the loyalty of his wife, Desdemona. And in so doing, he killed his wife for what he believed to be her disloyalty.

Laertes and Hamlet are friends in the play *Hamlet*. The conflict of loyalty to family versus friend causes Laertes to challenge his friend Hamlet. Laertes feels he must avenge his father's death at the hands of Hamlet. Before Laertes dies he asks Hamlet's forgiveness: "Exchange forgiveness with me, noble Hamlet. Mine and my father's death come not upon thee, Nor thine on me!"

Most famous friendships in history and literature are based on some kind of working relationship, proximity, or commitment to the same cause or ideology—for example, Caesar and Brutus, Boswell and Johnson, John the Baptist and Jesus, Sherlock Holmes and Dr. Watson, Susan B. Anthony and Elizabeth Cady Stanton.

A popular, well-known friendship that combines both shared work and proximity is the television show *Laverne & Shirley*. Experts say the appeal of that long-running television show is the friendship theme and especially the idea of women having a best friend. It illustrates in a hundred different ways the give-and-take relationship of best friends.

On the other hand, the show *The Odd Couple* pits two very different character types in a situation where they must learn to put up with each other, even though their life-styles are unusually different. They learn to accept each other, if not each other's way of life.

FAMOUS CHOICES

Have you ever wondered what famous person you might like for a friend? Some famous person in history? Or fiction?

Here are some of the choices given on a recent survey:

MERLIN THE MAGICIAN. He could help me perfect those things in my life that need improvement.

SISTER TERESA. She is a completely good person and is an inspiration to me.

WINNIE THE POOH. He was so lovable, even with all his faults. I just wanted to hug him all the time.

HAL PRINCE. It would be so exciting to have such a creative person for a friend. I could learn so much from him.

MOLIÈRE, THE FRENCH PLAYWRIGHT. He had the greatest sense of humor of any playwright I ever read. He saw all life as comedy.

Do you think you would have liked Socrates for a friend? Madame Curie, Winston Churchill, Albert Schweitzer, or Harriet Tubman? Maybe you would have liked Mark Twain, Eleanor Roosevelt, John F. Kennedy, or Katharine Cornell.

Take a look at items 1 to 6 below. Do you recognize any of these famous historical or fictional characters? Which one do you think you would like as a friend? Read the character sketch and select the one who appeals to you as a friend. Turn to the key and see whom you selected.

WHOM WOULD YOU CHOOSE?

1. She was a Polish-French physicist and chemist. She obtained her doctorate in 1904 from the Sorbonne. In the same year, she became an assistant in her husband's laboratory. She collaborated on research with her husband and together they won the Nobel Prize for Physics in 1903. She became the first woman professor at the Sorbonne. After her husband's death, she continued to work alone and isolated a certain element and published a scientific classic on the subject in 1910. The following year she was awarded the Nobel Prize for Chemistry.

2. He was an artist, sculptor, and painter. He left notebooks with sketches of men and birds unsurpassed for their knowledge of anatomy at that time. His other interests were science, geology, botany, anatomy, architecture, and engineering. His notebooks and drawings reveal a mind of incredible profundity. Although he left little mark on the development of Italian painting, considering his supreme gifts, he influenced a great many people in the art world.

He joined a winning charm of temper and manners, a tact for all societies, and an aptitude for all accomplishments. He is remembered as the most perfect example of the Renaissance "complete man."

3. A French actress of immense charm and intensity, she was noted for her slim figure, dark eyes, and golden voice. She performed at the Comédie Française but became impatient with the group's tradition, so she started her own tours throughout the world. She became a legend in her own lifetime through her high spirits and unconventional behavior. She had a long and brilliant career that took her all over the world. Her mastery of acting techniques and her magnetic personality combined to create the image of the "grand actress." She was best in emotional melodramatic parts, but she was willing to try anything. She made nine triumphant tours to the United States and made some early movies here. In her later years, she often slept in a casket.

4. She was a black slave from the State of New York, whose first language was Dutch. She was the first black woman to use the law to bring her son back from a slave state to a free one, and to sue successfully for libel. She had a magnificent voice and traveled all over the country singing and preaching. Although she couldn't read the Bible or anything else, she claimed God spoke directly to her. Most of her life she had no money in her pocket and only the clothes on her back. She had a wit and wisdom that pulled her through many a dangerous situation. She met Presidents and was received in the U.S. Senate. She had a dream of the Government giving land out West to the freed slaves to farm for themselves. President Lincoln considered the plan before his assassination.

5. Although he came from a well-to-do family, highly placed with English royalty, he was often imprisoned for his religious beliefs. He was a Quaker who believed all men were brothers and lived his life accordingly. He sailed across the Atlantic on the good ship *Welcome*. When smallpox hit the group, he worked day and night nursing the sick. There were many hardships during the voyage and at one point his company and crew were ready to give up and turn back. He convinced them all to continue the voyage. He was an exceptional athlete. He won the respect of the Indians he found in the New World, and made a treaty with them that was never broken in his lifetime. He lived to see his dream of a "greene country town" become a reality as "The City of Brotherly Love."

6. He was a tall, slender, hawk-nosed detective who wore a deerstalker hat and an inverness cape. He solved his first case

while a twenty-year-old student at Oxford. After graduation, he became the world's first private detective, a vocation he followed for twenty-three years. Before agreeing to share lodgings with a friend, he confessed to certain shortcomings. "I get in the dumps at times, and don't open my mouth for days on end." He liked to play the violin and could play quite well. He possessed not only an excellent deductive power but also a giant intellect. Anatomy, chemistry, mathematics, British law, and literature were all areas of his expertise. An athletic body complemented his outstanding intelligence. He seemed taller than his six feet because he was so slim. He often astonished his friends with displays of strength and agility. He was a superb boxer, fencer, and singlestick player. He had many adventures and close bouts with death.

Could you identify any of the persons? Which one would you select for a friend? Look at the key below to see whom you chose.

Here are the names of the characters described:

1. Madame Marie Curie (1867–1934)
2. Leonardo da Vinci (1452–1519)
3. Sarah Bernhardt (1844–1923)
4. Sojourner Truth (1797–1883)
5. William Penn (1644–1718)
6. Sherlock Holmes (1854–?)

Now that you know the person you selected, is he or she still your choice? Did you choose a fictional or a real character? Did you select someone on the basis of the information given who would be compatible with you?

Some of the specific qualities that each of these characters had to offer in their friendship were:

1. Madame Marie Curie	Intelligence Loyalty There when needed
2. Leonardo da Vinci	Artistic ability Intelligence Versatility/wide variety of interests
3. Sarah Bernhardt	Attractiveness Spiritedness Adventuresomeness/willingness to take risks

4. Sojourner Truth	Sense of humor
	Compassion
	Determinedness
5. William Penn	Adventuresomeness
	Compassion
	Athletic ability
6. Sherlock Holmes (fictional)	Honesty
	Intelligence
	Versatility/wide variety of interests

YOUR QUALITIES

Which one of these persons might have chosen *you* for a friend? Is it the same one you picked? What are some of the qualities you could offer one of these persons in a friendship? Would you return some of the same qualities offered or would you offer others which they might value on the basis of what you know about them?

Francis Bacon said a friend can provide "peace in the affections and support of the judgment."

"Support of the judgment" offers validation to your opinion. That validation tells you that others agree with your perception of the world. It tells you that your values are right, that you have good judgment.

Everyone needs that kind of validation from society at times. One old friend sums it up this way: "I want a friend to hear my point of view and give it weight, to respect the information I put forth."

She paused thoughtfully for a moment. "I want a friend to take my advice sometimes. That's the validation for me that my perception of the world is worth something."

A drama therapist from Maryland says, "A friend to me is someone who believes in me even when I don't."

One eighty-six-year-old expert on life says, "A friend is someone you can express your feelings to without fear of criticism."

Even with so many definitions of *friend* and what it means to different people, one thing stands out: all of us are happiest when we have someone we consider a friend. We all want a friend, even those of us who don't have one.

Here is more on the subject from Samuel Johnson: "So many qualities are requisite to the possibility of friendship and so many accidents must concur to its rise and continuance, that the greatest

22

part of mankind content themselves without it and supply its place, as they can, with interest and dependence."

Henry David Thoreau put it this way: "The most I can do for my friend is simply to be his friend."

Friendships are like plants. First someone or something must plant a seed in the proper environment. If the existing conditions are right, and if the plant is cared for, it may bloom or even blossom. Just as the plant can bloom with the right care, so can a friendship. The trick is to discover what the needs are in a friendship to help it grow.

Some plants can grow in one kind of soil but not another, just as some friendships need a certain environment. Most friendships need an environment of safety and support at least within each person. Some friendships offer the environment of comfort and stability. Friendship is hard pressed to grow in an environment of suspicion and hostility, and very rarely can it make any progress in an environment of fear. It is not a wild thing that can grow by itself; it needs tending and constant care. The soil needs renewal to offer new nutrients to all that grows there. Honesty offers one of the best environments in which friendship can grow. When that element is part of the environment, combined with trust, it promotes the growth of friendship. Sunshine is to plants what caring is to human beings. We soak it in and let it become part of us.

Every living thing needs time and space to grow, just as friendship does. It cannot be bought or sold. It can only be given freely and received joyously. Friendship is the most valuable asset in the world.

"Without friendship life is nothing." (A Latin proverb.)

CHAPTER 2

Different Kinds of Friendships

Friendships can be found everywhere. All it takes is a willingness to reach out or to be receptive to another's reach. Then you can accept what is offered if you choose. That offer could be to share a few minutes or an hour of your life or the beginning of a lifetime friendship. The first step in any relationship is accepting the hand that is held out.

Just as each of us has many sides to the self, we are attracted by various traits in other people. For that reason, we like a variety of characteristics in different people.

No one person can meet all the needs of any other person. Once you understand that, you open the door to a variety of other people and appreciate what they have to give. It may be someone to work with, someone to talk to, or simply someone for company.

Cicero said, "Nature has so formed us that a certain tie unites us all, but this tie becomes stronger from proximity."

Simply being at the same place at the same time prompted such famous friendships in fiction as Tom Sawyer and Huckleberry Finn, the Odd Couple—Felix and Oscar—or the cartoon pair Mutt and Jeff.

Usually we are attracted to people who are not completely different from us in every way. Although there is some truth in the old saying, "Opposites attract," more often than not there is some similarity. Usually those opposites are merely on the superficial level. There are similarities of values or standards. Even when two persons appear to be very different on the outside, there is some common denominator present, such as similar goals or outlook on life. The people we are attracted to share something in common with us.

We all set patterns that work for ourselves, but sometimes we forget how growth and change will influence those patterns. We keep doing things in the old ways instead of experimenting with the new. As we grow older, most of us take fewer risks. We stick with what we know.

When you were a child, another kid in the playground was your friend because he was there. Maybe you waited until someone asked you to play or you asked to join someone else's game. That's how children's friendships usually begin. Kids at the same place at the same time share the company. There is no problem of finding any similarity. Just being there is enough.

If you ever changed schools when you were young, you remember that churning feeling in your stomach when you walked into a new room filled with people you had never seen before. You felt a mixture of anticipation and fear. You desperately wanted someone to say "Hey, be my friend!" At the same time, you knew you must be careful about who would be your friend. If you accepted the outcast or the oddball as a friend, the other kids would stay away, figuring you chose your own kind. To them you showed poor judgment and they would label you an oddball until you could prove otherwise.

As an adult, when you move to a totally new situation, you must evaluate and be selective with people who reach out to you. You must be able to accept in a friendly way, or reject in a friendly way.

CHOICES

In today's world we all have an increased number of choices in our friends and in the kinds of friendships we pick. With mobility, both geographically and socially, our selections are vastly enlarged. Since most of us operate in several different worlds, we come in contact with a wide variety of individuals. In fact, many of our associations cross cultural, ethnic, and social boundaries. Therefore, we must practice selectivity with the types of friendships we formulate.

In our grandparents' time, grandfather had his family, his neighbors, his job. In grandmother's world, it was her family and her neighbors, and that was it. We have the same choices that were available to our grandparents plus dozens more.

Think about the people and places you contact. For example, you have opportunities to meet people in several of the following areas:

1. Home and family
2. Neighborhood
3. On the job or in school
4. Job- or school-related events or interests
5. Church, synagogue, or religious group or related ones
6. Recreational interest
   a. Swim club
   b. Tennis club
   c. Golf club
   d. Health spa
   e. Bridge club
   f. Garden club
   g. Others
7. Sports interest
   a. Team play
   b. Spectator/fan
   c. Booster club
   d. Individual competition
8. Sorority or fraternity interest
9. Service—past, present
10. Community groups
11. Hobby or special interest
12. Professional groups
13. Community theaters
14. Music groups

Add to this list other categories in which you know people.

One urban sociologist states, "Everyone in the United States is removed from everyone else by only three people." That makes ours a small world indeed. And it adds to the possibility of having something in common with a majority of others. Add to the list intergenerational associates—a friend's mother or father, Great-Aunt Lulu—and you see what a small world it really is. With so many opportunities available to meet people and make friends, where do you start?

Look around. What type of person do you like? What types are you usually attracted to? We all practice our own kind of selection. We must. We choose different friends for different reasons just as we offer different facets of ourselves in a friendship.

We have every opportunity to find a compatible friend. We may like one thing about this person and something entirely different about that one. Some people are more able and willing to give their friendship than others. At certain times we make greater demands on our friends than we do at other times. We must be aware of their needs as well as our own. We need not expect from any one person what he or she cannot give. Therefore it may be necessary to select more than one person. Perhaps our needs can be met by several acquaintances rather than by just one friend.

OCCUPATIONAL FRIENDSHIPS

Occupational friendships are some of the easiest to have. This is not to say they are not some of the best. Many organizations promote such friendships to help the newcomer feel at home. However, more often than not, it's the individual who must reach out.

One young teacher says: "I like a friend I can share my work with, to talk over mutual concerns and problems. From there it's not hard to share more and to exchange confidences."

"When you work in the same place with a group of guys, you can always find a few who like to chew the fat over a beer or two, or watch a game on TV," says a foundry worker in Pennsylvania. "Those guys might not be my best friends, but they need to unwind just like I do. I need that companionship after a hard day's work. It's great for me."

"If you work someplace where you like the job a lot, you'll probably find someone else who likes the job for similar reasons," says a twenty-five-year-old office worker. "I have lots of friends at the office, but the ones I really like are the ones who feel safe about their jobs—that feeling carries over into other areas."

The military knows how to promote occupational friendships. It assigns an escort to each new officer who comes on the base. The escort shows the newcomer around and introduces him to others.

"Military families reach out," a former Air Force officer says. "All of us were 'the new kid on the block' at one time or another ourselves, so we all make the effort to help the newcomer."

Some corporations promote that kind of effort among their executives. When an executive is transferred, someone in the new locale takes him under his wing and shows him the ropes.

Some people just have a knack for helping newcomers. Nora is one such person. Here's how she does it:

NORA: This is my new neighbor, Vernice. She's from the Bahamas. This is Sally.
SALLY: Nice to meet you, Vernice.

VERNICE: How do you do.

NORA: Sally, you and Vernice have a lot in common, because you both have young children and both like music.

SALLY: How nice. Do you play an instrument?

VERNICE: Yes, I play the violin.

SALLY: Wonderful. I play the piano with a group once a week. We need a violinist. We'd love to have you join us.

VERNICE: That's very kind of you, and I'd really love to join you, but I have to find a baby-sitter first.

SALLY: Don't worry about that. I'll share my list with you.

In this case, Nora functioned as the one who took Vernice under her wing. She paved the way for Vernice by introducing her to Sally, who had a lot in common with the newcomer.

Some people try to help newcomers but don't have the same skill Nora did. Take George, for example:

GEORGE: This is Tim. He's new in our department. He's from Philadelphia but says he's a Mets fan anyway. This is Hal.

HAL: Hi, Tim, welcome to the city.

TIM: Hello, Hal.

GEORGE: You guys should have a lot in common.

HAL: A Mets fan, eh?

TIM: Yeah.

GEORGE: Well, you guys get to know each other. See you later.

This time, although George gave some information, he didn't give enough or stay long enough to see that Tim, the newcomer, really made any kind of connection. The information offered was too impersonal. This introduction was little more than just that.

Assigning a specific person to look after another is used in some schools and colleges, in sororities and fraternities, i.e., big sister, or big brother. It's done in many international exchange programs.

"It's the old buddy system from camp," a young college woman from Montana said about her junior year abroad. "When I got off the boat, Simone—she was the daughter of the family I lived with. Anyway, Simone was right there to meet me. She was there whenever I needed her, the whole year I was in France. It was great, except sometimes she was there even when I didn't need her.

"If she hadn't been so cute and tried so hard, she would have been a pain. I couldn't go anyplace without Simone. Even when I dated Pierre, it was a joke. Simone and her boyfriend double-dated with us. That's what I call togetherness. Simone really took her responsibility seriously—she was wonderful. I had a marvelous time and saw France as few tourists ever do."

She looked up thoughtfully. "But I wonder if Simone had as good a time? After all, she was responsible for me; she had all the responsibility."

CONVENIENCE FRIENDSHIPS

Convenience friendships hold an important place in the scheme of things. In Chapter 1, you saw that one of the qualities most people described about their friends was, "being there when you need them."

Simply "being there" describes the friendship of convenience. This is the kind of friendship most of our grandparents had. Certainly, our forefathers depended heavily upon their neighbors. Their survival depended on their friends and neighbors. There was very little distinction between the two. Indeed, everyone had to function as a friend and be ready to pitch in and help when the occasion arose.

In the family, the older children took care of the younger ones. One neighbor looked after another. Barn-raising, harvesting, and many other farm-related activities depended on communal help. Their survival depended on cooperation among the group, which was often widely dispersed over the miles. Such a support network provided a necessary and good way of life. However, because of our ever-increasing mobility, people don't depend on their neighbors for friendship as they once did.

Many people look back on those days with some envy. There was never any question of whom you could depend on. You depended on your neighbors, and they depended on you. That's all there was to it.

Still, a good neighbor is important to most people today. Even if we live in a highly mobile environment, where neighbors change frequently, most of us make an effort to know our neighbors. Even if it's simply a "Good morning" or "Nice day today" type of association, we still have that sense of feeling neighborly. There is some carryover of the mutual responsibility feeling, even if ever so slight.

Benjamin Franklin said, "Better a good neighbor next door than a brother a thousand miles away."

ORGANIZATIONAL FRIENDSHIPS

Churches and synagogues have long been sources for establishing friendships. They offer a central place for people with similar philosophies and/or theologies to come together. Most offer social activities as well, and although this also may lead to a friendship of convenience, it is a natural place to find others who share the same values.

There are many other special interest groups that offer a common meeting ground. School and community organizations offer a wide variety of people who come together for a purpose or cause. Often the only thing uniting these people is that cause, but again, being at the same place at the same time can promote friendship.

Lodge brothers and their sister organizations fulfill an important need in the lives of many. These groups offer their members a feeling of belonging to a larger community.

Groups such as community theatres, garden clubs, and fortnightly groups offer a sense of community and a sense of belonging to a special interest group. With membership in these groups, a certain sense of selectivity comes into play as well. Your interest is important. It is shared by other people who also think it is important.

Certain organizations, such as the armed services, promote a loyalty for the whole organization that lasts a lifetime. "Once a Marine, always a Marine," says a former member of the Marine Corps proudly. He went on to say: "I love the Marine Corps. When I was a Marine, there was no question of what you did when you needed help. You went to the Corps." This kind of devotion to an organization illustrates a different kind of friendship. This friendship carries over to any other person who is a member of that special group.

It's the same kind of brotherhood found in some fraternal orders and social organizations. Members of these groups are sorority *sisters*, fraternity or lodge *brothers*. They are members of a select, and often highly elite, group. Even if there are one or two members whom others would not choose for friends, the very fact they are brothers in this group dictates that all members are acceptable to all other members as friends. Members of such groups often wear some visible symbol proclaiming their membership, such as a pin or a ring. These symbols identify those who belong. Certain college and university graduates frequently wear a visible sign that proclaims their allegiance to the alma mater. These labels are easily identifiable to their members wherever, whenever they meet. The ring or the pin says clearly, "I belong to a special group."

"He's a Harvard man" or "He's a Yale man" say certain symbols. The orange-and-black scarf clearly identifies a Princeton man. These symbols help in identification in the Old Boys Network too. When applying for a job with a prestigious firm where intellect is highly prized, the man or woman who wears a Phi Beta Kappa key clearly has an edge.

Perhaps the most obvious symbol of belonging is the wedding ring. For years it was worn mostly by women, but nowadays it has become popular with men. Both men and women declare their nonavailability with their symbol, the wedding ring.

Within these categories of friendships, there are divisions in each such as: (1) woman-woman friendships, (2) man-man friendships, (3) man-woman friendships, (4) older-younger friendships, (5) student-teacher friendships.

WOMAN-WOMAN FRIENDSHIPS

Psychiatrists and behavioral scientists agree that most women find it easier to develop close, intimate friendships than do men. Women have traditionally been able to reach out, to nurture, to mother. Perhaps the very nature of their vulnerability has made it easier for them to risk that intimate level of friendship. It is easier to admit weakness when there is not as much to lose. The male counterpart may have a career or financial position to protect, or just his macho image.

Perhaps the fastest growing order of friendship is the woman-woman relationship. Woman's place in society has changed greatly in the past generation. Many women's needs are different today from what they were a generation ago. Today women are in transition, or what sociologists label "the transitional generation."

Nowadays most adult women don't have to be dependent on a man. They are concerned with providing for themselves. Many provide or help provide for their families as well. In the past, this role was held exclusively by men. Many of today's women are as independent as men have always been.

Your grandmother probably never worked outside the home. Most women today do work outside the home or will at some time during their lifetime. These women come in contact with a greater variety of people from all walks of life than their grandmothers ever did. That gives them more choices for associations, more options in life-styles.

Women are just beginning to realize they can have the same kind of "buddy-pal" relationship that men have taken for granted for years. But first, before a woman can be a friend to someone else, she must be her own person.

During the Renaissance, Orinda wrote about friendship among women. The word she used most often to describe a woman friend was "listener." She spoke of the forging of an "us."

The old taboo of girl-girl relationship is no longer valid. Years ago there was often a sexual connotation to such relationships. Women were afraid of an intimate friendship for fear that people would think of them as homosexual. It was not so with men, however. The glories of the undying friendship of man for man have been heralded since the beginning of time. Today, women can have this same kind of comradely friendship.

As far back as the Golden Age of Greece, Sappho alone wrote of female friendships. She wrote of the "good feelings" among females in many different relationships, especially the mother-daughter one.

Traditionally, men have not shown their feelings. A show of emotion was considered unmasculine, while women, on the other hand, have been encouraged to demonstrate their affections.

"Women have always been able to touch and hug to the envy of many a man," offers the dean of women at a Pennsylvania college. "Women, by the very nature of how they have been brought up, find it easier to achieve intimacy in friendship."

"Mature, whole people make the best friends," a psychiatrist from Philadelphia says.

Relationships that work are those in which both participants help each other to be individuals, to belong to themselves.

MAN-MAN FRIENDSHIPS

Man-man friendships have inspired endless tales of heroism and self-sacrifice. More men are put in strife situations: contact sports, war, hazardous or dangerous work, adventurous living.

"When you're in a strife situation, you get down to the core of people much quicker," a thirty-six-year-old athletic coach explains.

Wartime buddies are a good example of how these man-man relationships occur quickly. "You're in an interdependent situation," says a former Air Force navigator. "You learn fast which people you can count on and which you can't. Sometimes your life depends on it. Even those friendships which are tremendously important then, most of them are temporary and not meaningful on a long-range basis. But they serve a necessary purpose at the time."

Most men have a hard time with the intimate or deepest level of friendship. When they share thoughts and ideas, dreams and goals, they share areas of vulnerability. They admit weakness. And to admit weakness—in the eyes of most men—is to invite destruction. Men often choose to remain at a distance rather than risk intimacy. Men are much more comfortable in "doing" relationships. Perhaps they reach their own level of intimacy by that path rather than the "talking" way.

At any rate, man-man friendships are the ones most people think of when friendship is discussed. More has been written about the brotherhood of man than any other kind of relationship except love, and even that is often equated with the love of *mankind*.

MAN-WOMAN FRIENDSHIPS

Of all the different types of friendships, friendship between a man and a woman is the most controversial. Many experts feel such a relationship is possible only if each of the individuals respects the other as a human being first. Each must be secure within his or her own gender. In such a relationship the ground rules have to be clearly stated in the beginning. Both parties must be honest about their needs and/or expectations in the friendship. If either the man or the woman enters the friendship hoping it will turn into a different relationship, one or the other is in for trouble.

"There are times when I would like a man friend," says a young woman recently graduated from college. "But I am engaged and plan to be married in June. I make that fact clear. I let the man know what kind of relationship it will be. I never mislead anyone. It's so easy for someone to delude himself if he wants the relationship to be something more. If the man can accept my friendship on a platonic basis, fine. I will be a good friend. If not, well . . . I'll find another friend who will."

A woman doctor in Pennsylvania, who says some of her best friends are men, gives this advice: "Man-woman friendships are possible only if the man does not view the woman as a sexual object."

Another doctor, who proclaims he's a male chauvinist and proud of it, disagrees. "Man-woman friendships are just not possible. Man is an animal. Friendship creates closeness, and proximity causes sexual problems. There's no way around it.

"The policeman's wife who objects to her husband having a female partner is smart. A man and a woman in such close proximity can only cause problems. Both parties may be sorry afterward, if they succumb to temptation, but it happens. If they hadn't been forced into that closeness leading to a sexual attraction, the relationship would not have occurred. The only way a man-woman friendship can exist is when the woman is really more male than female."

A forty-year-old newspaperwoman says: "Now that women are in business, man-woman friendships are more likely to occur. Both parties have much more to talk about. It's not easy, but it can be worked out." She paused for a moment and then added a final comment: "For years women have made better friends than men because they've had more time to work at friendship."

One of the most important elements in any friendship is respect. When that essential element of respect exists between any two persons, it is possible to build a friendship. Everyone has the capacity to care about many different kinds of people. The man or woman who can look at the opposite sex as just another human being has opened up the other 50 percent of society from which to choose friends.

OLDER-YOUNGER FRIENDSHIPS

Older-younger friendship is the relationship in which we all begin life. It is the easiest to accept in the early stages. For many of us it is the only relationship we know until school begins. Mother or father is the role model. If the parent is absent and/or another adult comes into our life, that person is the role model. At some point as youngsters we select a role model outside our family—someone we admire and want to emulate.

Everyone has role models. Sometimes we give those role models superhuman qualities. We put them on a pedestal. When the realization comes that these favorite neighbors, teachers, coaches, choir directors, scout leaders are human beings after all, then—and only then—can the relationship change and continue on a different level. With this kind of friendship, both parties must accept the growth and change. This is the hardest part of maintaining that relationship. The relationship between mentor and neophyte is a classic example of the apprentice system. It is the method by which all arts and crafts were learned in early times.

34

Many older people see themselves in the young neophyte. Others want to give a helping hand up the ladder. Still others are more concerned with sharing their art than the person they share it with.

STUDENT-TEACHER FRIENDSHIPS

Teachers traditionally play the role of mentor. It is the wise teacher who knows when to change his or her role of mentor for that of equal. It is one of the greatest joys any teacher can have—when the pupil has learned enough to be an equal.

One former high school and college football player comments on how much his coach's friendship has meant to him over the years: "There are four or five of us left from that old championship team. We played all four years of high school on the coach's team. We've been through a lot of trials together to create a special bonding relationship. We get together several times a year with the coach. He loves it, and so do we. I'm almost fifty now, so you know how long this relationship has lasted. It's very special."

Most people know how to maintain a relationship when their specific role is clearly defined, either younger or older. It's fairly simple when the role is specified in the relationship: teacher to pupil, mother to child, boss to worker. One role is the supplicant, the disciple; the other is the wise leader.

The difficulty occurs in these relationships when the time comes to make the transition from either position to bring it into a lateral relationship, an equal friendship. Sometimes this transition is impossible. Then comes a choice: Do I want to retain this relationship even though I will always be the student?

Some people are quite willing to remain the student forever to continue the relationship. Others are eager for a more lateral relationship. They never forget what the mentor has taught them, how much their universe has been expanded, or how far they have come; they have reached another level of maturity. The persons who recognize this in themselves are anxious for the mentor to see it also. Unfortunately, some mentors are never able to see it.

One of the most rewarding and meaningful experiences is when the mentor realizes that the student is no longer a student, that he or she has matured to the level of being an equal. This can be a grand sharing time for both. It can be a continuous growing relationship. This can occur regardless of the ages of those concerned. Physical age has very little to do with being equal in the life of the mind.

A housewife in Indiana says: "I have a lot of older friends. I think that stems from the relationship with my mother. We've been good friends for most of my adult life. Somewhere in my twenties the transition occurred. We were both able to make the changeover from the parent-child relationship to being friends on an equal basis."

From there she went on to say that she sees many of the parents of her former friends who no longer live nearby. "Some of the older people here are from my former life. They were a part of my growing up. I'm glad I'm able to give my help when it's needed."

There is something very special about a relationship that can be successful through the transition to a lateral friendship. More often than not, it comes from the older person who sees the potential for the equal relationship. The older one can encourage the transition when the time is right.

SUPPORT SYSTEMS

Everyone needs different kinds of friendships. We need support systems. There may be one person you like to bowl with, another who sings in the choir with you, another who enjoys going to the theatre. Someone else may be a sympathetic listener. With a little effort you can find someone to share many different areas of your life. You can develop your own support system. Many people create an extended family of friends.

One such person was Margaret. Margaret's own family had grown up and moved away. Her only grandchild was in college, also far away. When Margaret's husband died, she thought she had nothing more to live for, no one to care for or to care about her. She had no skills for the marketplace. She had been a homemaker all her life.

What Margaret did was to get involved with the Foster Grandparent Program. Margaret became the Foster Grandmother to a young woman who had been labeled an "emotionally disturbed" teenager. She was so successful with that relationship that she took on four more "difficult" teenaged girls.

Margaret is as happy as can be. She has people to love and care about, and those people love and care about her. She found something she does well. "All those girls need is someone to love them with no strings attached—just to love them for who they are—I'm good at that!"

36

Support groups come in all categories. You don't have to go to the extreme that one young woman went to: "I don't even drink but I went to an Alcoholics Anonymous meeting just to find people to talk to."

Look around you. There are groups for every interest: classes that teach every skill desired, continuing education classes, special interest groups, Great Books discussions. You can find "a listening ear" any number of places. And, when you learn to be a listening ear yourself, you'll find people galore.

There are many different kinds of friendships. Start by looking around where you are. Broaden your base to include your interests. Remember the words of one Greek scholar, who reminds us that "a certain tie unites us all."

Keep in mind what Mark Twain said, "Nothing so needs reforming as other people's habits."

Learn to accept the limitations of others. Learn to accept the various kinds of friendships people are willing to give, then you will always find someone who is willing to share a friendship. If you can accept what others are willing to give, instead of what you want from them, you will always find someone to share wherever you are. You will develop your own support system.

SIX DO'S AND DON'TS
TO DEVELOP YOUR OWN SUPPORT SYSTEM

Do look for different qualities in different people.
Don't expect any one person to answer all your needs in
    friendship.

Do accept and enjoy what people have to offer.
Don't expect people to give what they cannot or will not give.

Do accept the limitations of others.
Don't expect others to respond exactly as you would.

Do offer only what you are willing to give.
Don't think you must give all or nothing.

Do realize your time and friendship is precious.
Don't try to give it to everyone.

Do keep trying.
Don't give up if you don't succeed immediately.

CHAPTER 3

Testing Yourself: What Is Your Friendship Quotient?

> If a man does not make new acquaintances as he advances through life, he will soon find himself left alone. A man, sir, should keep his friendship in constant repair.
>
> —*Samuel Johnson*

It's not enough to know what a friend is or the many different kinds of friendships. What most people really want to know is: How do I fit into the scheme of things? Do I have a good friend? Am I a good friend? They want to know their friendship quotient (F.Q.). Many people feel they give more in a friendship than they receive; they are the "givers." Others receive more than they give; they are the "takers."

Some people are very careful about giving friendship.

"Once I've given it, it's irrevocable," says a public relations director in New York. "It's like the difference between a flirtation and a love affair."

A twenty-five-year-old political activist says, "I think I have more to offer most people than most people have to offer me."

On the other hand, a young woman asks: "Why do I feel like I always get more than I give? I try, I really do, but my friends are all 'doers.' I'm attracted to those superego types, the achievers. Most of the time, I feel like I'm along for the ride."

Some people don't realize that simply be being there they can offer a supportive presence or a listening ear that can be as important as many other qualities. Different people bring a variety of components to a friendship. Oftentimes individuals don't realize exactly what they give to a relationship or what they want from it.

All people need someone they can trust, someone they can count on. A friend doesn't care about inconvenience or if he does, the inconvenience is minor to the friendship. Most people look for some of the same qualities in other people that they have.

"I value in other people what I bring in a friendship. I want some of those same elements back," explains Margie from Chicago.

Look over the following list of qualities. Pick out the ten you consider the most significant to you, the ten you most often look for or find in a friend. Which qualities are most important to your relationships?

QUALITIES IN FRIENDSHIP

loyalty	interest
truthfulness	honesty
sincerity	common interests
sense of humor	values and standards
optimism	good listener
sensitivity	sympathy
intelligence	attractiveness
kindness	tolerance
patience	independence
compassion	understanding
dependability	consistency
availability	fun-loving
empathy	outgoingness
energy	enthusiasm

After you have selected the ten you value most in a friend, look at the list again. What are the ten qualities you bring to a friendship? Remember, choose only ten and be honest with yourself. Choose ten assets you already have for friendship, not the qualities you would like to have.

If you selected similar characteristics both times, your friends are probably very much like you. You look for people similar to yourself for friends. If you picked different qualities each time, you like people who are different from you.

Michael, a director, says: "A friend is one who lacks the qualities and attributes that I have but who is in harmony with me. He brings different qualities than I have. And I offer the same complementary elements. I bring to him or her those qualities that person doesn't have. In this way we learn from each other. That's an important part of any relationship."

This director from Long Island goes on to say, "We must share the ability to confide in each other with the belief that neither of us will ever break that confidence or use any confidential information against the other."

When a friend sees you as an incredible source of strength, there is something about that belief or faith that causes you to rise to the occasion—or at least to try.

On the other hand, some people do not allow you to give what you would like in a relationship. They stop you before you start.

"I can't stand people who say, 'I can't let you do that for me.' I treasure people who let me do for them. When they say, 'I can't let you do that,' it means they think they'll be asked for a return. I don't expect any return. I simply want to *do* for the people I care about," offers a woman named Midge.

Many of us see ourselves one way, while our friends see us another. We must bridge that difference with some kind of connection.

MAKING CONNECTIONS

Recognize the importance of a connection. Not everyone can make it in the same way. One woman tells the story of her aunt who lives several hundred miles away.

"She sends me newspaper clippings. Sometimes she writes a sentence or two on a note which she includes, but not always. If I took these communications on their surface value, it would mean very little. I had to grow up before I realized this is her way of keeping in touch—of making a connection. What she is telling me is 'I'm thinking of you.' "

There is a Pennsylvania Dutch saying that offers this comment:

> Too soon old
> Too late smart.

We all need to find ways to make connections with other people. Recognize the value of the connection; be sensitive to the person who wants to communicate with you but is not on your wavelength. And recognize the value of small talk as an attempt at that connection. A great deal of "filler" time among friends is spent in small talk.

In vaudeville they used to say, "Vamp 'til ready."

That meant keep the time step going if you were dancing, or keep talking if you were the M.C. or announcer. You filled the time until the star or guest of honor came. In other words, keep the audience entertained, keep the connection going. Don't say anything important, just say something—until the next attraction comes on. That

40

kind of "vamping 'til ready" is to the stage what small talk is to making the connection. No one can talk about earth-shattering issues all the time. Hence, small talk is the filler.

There are times when we say, "It's a nice day, isn't it?" But what we really want to know is whether someone else perceives the universe the same way we do.

Some people feel that small talk is a waste of time. Most relationships start on that level. It is a nonpersonal, noncommittal, nonthreatening beginning. Even though you may feel you'd rather not spend time at it, remember there are other people who start a relationship that way. Consequently, look behind the words for the connection.

AVAILABILITY

Some people are more open to friendship, both old and new, than others. Not everyone would agree with Johnson's words at the beginning of this chapter.

"I don't have time in my life for new friendship," explains a thirty-eight-year-old executive. "I can't afford to squander my time. It's all I can do to make room in my life for those relationships which have stood the test of time. I can't reach out or be receptive to anyone else."

Right now this executive has a low F.Q. A year from now it might change. But at this moment he is a poor candidate for anyone who reaches out for his friendship.

"I'm moving to Texas soon," offers a twenty-three-year-old management trainee. "I look forward to meeting new people and making new friends. Luckily I'm good at the 'getting to know you game.' It's always been easy for me to suggest, 'Let's do something together.' "

Obviously this young woman's F.Q. is high. Not only is she eagerly looking forward to her new experience, but she has confidence in her own ability to do well in the situation. This confidence comes from previous successes in what she calls the "getting to know you game."

"I'm too old to worry about new friends," says a retired salesman. "When you get older, you don't reach out as much. I play cards with some guys once a week. That's good enough. Sometimes those guys get awfully boring. It's the same old stuff all the time. But what can I do? You can't advertise for new friends. And if you did, who'd apply?"

This salesman's F.Q. is not as high as the young woman's, but it's not as low as the executive's. Obviously he doesn't know where or how to make the effort himself. But if the opportunity presented itself, he would be receptive to someone else who reached out to him.

"I'd love to meet some new people," says a thirty-eight-year-old chemist, "but when . . . and how? My world is this laboratory and the people who work here. We're all interested in the project we're working on, but that's all we have in common or talk about. I like to swim, hike, birdwatch, but all those things I do alone. My best friend . . . " He paused for a moment and chuckled to himself. "Who am I kidding? He's my only friend. We trained together, but he's on the other side of the country now. We rarely see each other."

He stopped, probing his own feelings analytically, then added, "Besides, I'm really more interested in chemistry than people."

Finding the F.Q. here is more complicated. Af first the chemist said he would like to meet new people, but the things he likes to do are all things he can do alone. He admits later that he cares more about chemistry than people. Obviously this man would need a strong attraction to be receptive to anything more than just an acquaintance.

Each time you reach out for a new friend or open yourself to another's outreach, you take a risk. You risk rejection. You risk neglect. You risk getting involved and being abandoned or involved in a destructive relationship. Nevertheless, when you find a friend, those risks are well worth the effort.

FINDING OUT YOUR FRIENDSHIP QUOTIENT

Everyone has different levels of readiness for friendship. Some people are perfectly happy with the relationships that already exist in their lives. Other people are always open to new people and new relationships. Find out what your F.Q. is.

How are you at the friendship game? What kind of F.Q. do you have? Excellent, good, average, or low? The following questions will give you your level. Answer the twenty-five questions below with YES, NO, or SOMETIMES. Then turn to the key to find out your F.Q.

FRIENDSHIP QUOTIENT TEST

Answer with a Y for YES, N for NO, and S for SOMETIMES.

1. Do you think you are a lovable person? ____
2. Do you look forward to meeting new people? ____
3. Can you make small talk even though it bores you? ____
4. Can you support your friend's choice even though you think it's wrong? ____
5. Can you keep another's confidence when it is to your benefit to repeat it? ____
6. Do you make an effort to keep in touch with friends you don't see often? ____
7. Can you do favors for a friend without expecting something in return? ____
8. Can you listen to others without offering comments unless asked? ____
9. Do you feel the need to agree with your friends to please them? ____
10. Do you think friendship has to be earned? ____
11. Do you expect a certain reciprocity in a friendship? ____
12. Do you understand when your friend is too busy to see you? ____
13. Can you take time to cultivate new friends? ____
14. Can you give up something to be with a friend? ____
15. Can you walk away when a friend says or does something to hurt you and not be easily offended? ____
16. Do you respect your ability to make a good judgment? ____
17. Can you still support your friend even though he let you down? ____
18. Do you go along with another's plans even when you'd rather not? ____
19. Can you start a conversation with a stranger? ____
20. Can you be a friend with someone you know is surpassing you? ____

21. Can you deal with a friend's criticism of you?   ____
22. Do you find yourself an interesting person?   ____
23. Can you remain loyal when your loyalty is proven wrong?   ____
24. Can you accept it when your friend is not available when you need him?   ____
25. Can you laugh at yourself when you have made a bad choice?   ____

First, add the total number of Y's. Three S's equal one Y. If you answered YES to 20 or more questions, your F.Q. is EXCELLENT; 15 or more, GOOD; 10 or more, AVERAGE; fewer than 10, LOW, meaning you're really not interested in new friends or nurturing old relationships.

Do you give more than you get in a friendship? If you answered YES to questions 3, 4, 6, 7, 9, 12, 14, 17, 18, 21, 24, you probably give more than you get in return. If you answered YES to questions 1, 10, 11, 16, 22, 25 and NO to questions 3, 9, 14, 23, the chances are you get more than you give. Most of us fall somewhere in between.

Think about the people you know, friends or acquaintances you'd like for friends. Are you the same with each person, or do you offer different facets of yourself to different people? How often have you said or heard, "She brings out the best in me"? Have you ever felt, I'm richer for having known him or her?

Some people demand or inspire a high level of performance or achievement from friends. Some simply accept whatever others are willing to give. Still others act as a catalyst to bring out the best in everyone.

"I have a friend I've known for over thirty years," says a writer from Detroit. "I first knew her in the student-teacher relationship. We moved to the lateral friendship years ago. This woman not only inspires me but also gives me the supportive feeling that I can *do* something important. I highly respect her criticism. Sometimes I don't see her for a year, but she always challenges me. After I've been with her for an hour or so, I feel like my batteries are recharged. I want to blaze new trails, to strive for a richer experience and improve my work. She is the most honest person I've ever known. She never says something is good if she doesn't believe it is. I've never known anyone with such total honesty."

On the other hand, people can bring out your bad qualities as well as the good—unfortunate, but true. When you find yourself doing something that is inconsistent with your value system, that is a destructive relationship. When one of you feels she has to go along with the other, even though she knows it is wrong for her, that is a destructive or toxic relationship.

If the interchange that goes on between two persons makes one of them feel crummy, it's time to get out. In a true friendship, one does not give up the responsibility to one's "I," or self. Other kinds of destructive relationships simply erode another's well-being.

Some people find it much easier to criticize what they don't like than to praise what they do like.

"I stay away from negative people," a young dental hygienist says. "People who always complain depress me. And who wants to be depressed all the time?"

Negative people aren't happy unless they find negative aspects of a situation and point it out to others. On the other hand, there are those people who find the positive aspects of the situation. Positive people come in a variety of shapes and personalities.

Here are six profiles. Read these profiles and select the one you would choose for a friend.

PROFILES

Sunshine Sally is always happy and cheerful, fun to be with and do things with. She can talk about people and things. She's attractive and sees the positive side of almost everything.

Confident Cal is good-looking, athletic. He's good at games and sports. He likes to do things in groups, but he's not much of a talker. He has lots of male friends and acquaintances.

Intelligent Ida enjoys good conversation and likes to discuss ideas, philosophy, politics, etc. She has a strong sense of self. She shows good judgment and offers advice when asked.

Humorous Harry has a good sense of humor. He enjoys a variety of activities. He's outgoing and likes people. He's basically optimistic and enjoys a good laugh, especially on himself.

Perfect Penny is intelligent, loyal, honest, and has a good sense of humor. She is warm and outgoing, a good conversationalist and a good listener. She has a variety of interests and has sound standards and values.

Dependable Dan is there when you need him, a good listener with a sympathetic ear. He's always ready to lend a helping hand. He's interested in a lot of things and genuinely cares about people.

All these profiles offer positive characteristics. Moreover, the one you choose will tell you something about your own priorities. It will show you what attracts you most in a friend. If you choose Perfect Penny, however, you may be expecting too much. It's possible to find all those qualities in one person, but not very likely. Don't pass up other people who have only some of the qualities in your search for the perfect friendship.

STEREOTYPES

Names. Everyone has certain stereotypes about people. These stereotypes can be a hindrance to friendship or a help. Mark Twain had a fondness for a certain name. "I never met a Judy I didn't like," he said.

Like Mark Twain, many of us have stereotypes in the connotation of names. You may have known a Fanny you disliked. Every time you meet another Fanny, she has two strikes against her. You may remember your family or friends who talked about awful Emma.

How can you dislike someone named Hap or Joy? Holly and Rose conjure images of nature as well as of people.

Look at the list of names below and see if you have an instant like or dislike for any of them. Examine the stereotypes you have in your mind about them.

Bertha	Sam	Jack	Tina
Ben	Sarah	Jane	Tim
Percy	Abe	David	Warren
Patsy	Abigail	Della	Winnie

Other Stereotypes. If we have stereotypes about names, what kinds do we have about nationalities, religions, physical appearances, vocations, life-styles? Take a look at these stereotypes. Do you agree with any of them? What are some of your own? Do any of these lines sound familiar?

"All Californians are hippies."
"All men with beards have weak jaws."
"All New Yorkers are unfriendly."
"All long-haired men are dirty."
"All doctors are cold-blooded."
"All Italians love opera."
"All career women are unfeminine."
"All used-car salesmen are liars."
"All divorced women are looking for another man."
"All blondes have more fun."

46

What it takes to break a stereotype is to bring it out into the light and examine it logically. Think of all the exceptions to the stereotypes above. Once you've done that, you can see how ridiculous most of them are. You don't want a latent stereotype image to interfere with a new friendship. When you get rid of those old images, you open up new avenues for associations. Erase the blackboard of your own mind with those stereotypes. Now you have a nice clean slate for all kinds of new relationships.

BEST AND WORST

Some friendships seem better for you than others. One person inspires you to do your best work while another lets you get away with the least effort possible. Others are content with no effect either way. Some friends spur you on with the spirit of competition. For others, it's too much effort.

Your friends can benefit you in other ways too. In fact, the Old Boys Network and more recently the New Girls Network are good examples of how friends help each other in business. College alumni frequently use the same system to help their own.

Just as these networks offer support for their members, other types of relationships take some commitment also. Although nurturing a friendship takes time and effort, sometimes effort is not enough. Frequently, one party grows and changes, and the other does not. Not everyone does change and grow in the same way. Few persons do it at the same time or to the same degree.

Consequently, when one person stays at the same level, and the other moves forward, it can be threatening to the one who is stationary. Some individuals view any change as a threat. A variety of life forces cause changes in people.

"Ambition can change people also. When they become terribly ambitious, the relationship changes, so I don't want to continue the friendship," comments a writer from Tennessee.

Just as you've heard the line, "She brings out the best in me," the reverse is true also. There are people who "bring out the worst in me."

Whether the worst is a flaring temper, anger, or whatever, chances are you use negative energy to deal with that factor. If you find yourself dealing with an emotional incident over and over in your head long after it has occurred, your thoughts and energies are working in a nonproductive manner; that is negative energy. That kind of reliving an emotional trauma after it is finished can serve no useful purpose. It will result in the same agitated emotional state that you suffered when the incident occurred. It can only erode your well-being.

CONTINUED GROWTH

Consequently, friendships that continue to grow are those in which both parties are open to new experiences and learning, new people and understanding. These friends continue to bring new insight and feeling to the relationship; they continue to expand their universe.

In brief, when friends continue to grow, they stay open for new experiences and new people. They keep their F.Q. at least on the good level. These people with good F.Q.'s take their friendships seriously and give them some thought. In fact, no matter what your F.Q., you can raise it with some effort and understanding. What most of us desire is a friend, to have and to be.

An architect named Don, with an excellent F.Q., sums it up this way:

"I take friendship very seriously. Friendship is the same as a love relationship. It is a serious interaction between two persons. It takes a lot of work. That's probably something people don't understand about friendship.

"Why are you friends with certain people? What do you expect to get out of it?

"A relationship for me has to be based on *my* giving to the other person my friendship. I'm not concerned with give-and-take. Barter is for business—not friendship. You can't *owe* a friend a favor. You do for friends because you want to—because they're friends."

Consequently, in order for you to be the best friend possible, you have to become the best or most complete person you can. Mature, whole people make the best friends.

48

CHAPTER 4

What to Look For in a Friend

There is no friend like an old friend who has shared our morning days, no greeting like his welcome, no homage like his praise.   —*Oliver Wendell Holmes*

The virtues of friendship have been praised in great drama, oratory, and every literary form more often than any other virtue except love. Indeed, the Latin word for friendship, *amicitia*, is derived from the word for love—*amor*. Rightly so, since both love and friendship declare that two persons share themselves with each other.

And while you may have one great love or perhaps several in your lifetime, you can have an untold number of friends over that same period of time.

An epigram on friends says:

Friends are like melons. Shall I tell you why?
To find one good, you must a hundred try.

Just as friendship occurs on many different levels, the word *friend* calls up many different images. For some of us, it brings forth a memory of a childhood friend long since gone, a college roommate, or a wartime buddy. Often it's someone with whom we shared an important time in our life, usually involving some kind of "growing" experience.

For other people the word *friend* merely brings to mind a television pair like Laverne and Shirley, or Felix and Oscar.

With some, it is a fantasy image. That imagined character is all they ever had of their ideal of "the one true friendship."

"I am very comfortable with the friends I have," offers a newspaperwoman in New Jersey. "For the ideal friend, I wouldn't know where to look. Someone like Mark Twain must have been a great friend. He was funny and frank, always interesting. One thing is sure, you'd never be bored with Mark Twain for a friend."

49

For most of us, when we think of a friend we think of a pal we see every day or frequently.

Remember what Francis Bacon said about the friend who can provide "peace in the affections and support of the judgment."

Friends offer a validation to your judgment. If the person you choose for a friend reciprocates, it is a way of endorsing your unique worth as a human being. Your expectations have been met.

EXPECTATIONS

Your judgment plays a big part in your selection of the persons you choose for friends. If your expectations are too high, you may never find the perfect friend. On the other hand, if your expectations are too low, and you offer your friendship to any and all who come along, you might never experience the "affections" that Francis Bacon refers to.

Some people are afraid to risk the emotional commitment in friendship. If they don't get involved, they don't get hurt. Their defense for the avoidance of pain is to repel anyone who may become too close.

A person who sees the world with suspicion, and questions the motives of others, perceives the world in a way that keeps others away.

Friendship doesn't just happen, someone makes it happen. It takes time and effort on both sides. Friends are expected to do things together, to do things for each other. There are certain demands each person feels free to make on the other. Friendship is emotionally demanding and time-consuming.

Many people go through life with acquaintances rather than friends, because they don't recognize the potential for friendship in others or recognize their own needs in the relationship. In other words, they don't know how to read the signals from a potential friend, so their relationship remains on the same level. It never advances past the acquaintance stage.

SMALL TALK

Here's where the value of small talk comes in. Listen to the signals you receive. Take the risk and ask some questions that can move the conversation from the small-talk level to a deeper one. Don't be afraid to be the one who asks the questions. Think of each human being as an original, unique creation. If the other person signals his discomfort with deeper level questions, pull back and stay with the filler or small talk.

Don't overlook the shy or retiring person. Sometimes his or her signals for friendship are slower in coming than others'. With some introspective personalities, you must make the extra effort—DIG— to get them to open up. Remember the old saying, "Still water runs deep."

Stop for a minute and think about what *you* mean by the word *friend*. You've seen several definitions in previous chapters. One of the dictionary definitions was "a person attached to another by feelings of affection or personal regard." There's that word *affection* again. Most people agree that *friendship* is on a level beyond preliminary association.

"Friendship is undefinable. You can experience it. You can identify it. You know when it's there and when it's not there," explains Louise, a psychology teacher.

It's not logical. As educators say, it's not *cognitive*, it's *affective*.

"You cannot intellectualize friendship any more than you can intellectualize love. When you have it, you're happy. When you don't, you're miserable," affirms an education writer named Marjorie.

SIX LEVELS OF FRIENDSHIP

Some of you remember a film with the late Ingrid Bergman called *The Inn of the Sixth Happiness*. Perhaps friendship can be viewed like that, with six levels:

Level 1. Someone to talk to
Level 2. Someone to play or work with
Level 3. Someone to count on
Level 4. Someone to share mutual experiences and special times with
Level 5. Someone to share thoughts and ideas; life of the mind
Level 6. Someone to trust who will respect and support you and your growth

Almost all associations begin on the first or second level. Most of us want and/or need someone with whom we can share our lives on either the fifth or sixth level of friendship. But, for many people, the gap between the fourth and fifth level is a chasm too wide to breach. The fear of rejection will not allow them to take the giant step necessary to move from one level to the other.

Here's where the fear of taking a risk or the fear of rejection creates an insurmountable barrier. Some people fear the imagined danger of human intimacy. They are afraid to trust. If they move tc a deeper level of friendship, they must give more of themselves and accept more from another. That giving and accepting could bring about a change. The fear of change is the fear of the unknown, which is even more threatening than rejection.

Each of the preliminary levels of friendship must be carefully worked through before the fifth can be reached. Here is the level that takes effort and sharing of self from both participants. One person cannot do it alone. To reach this level you must choose someone who is receptive to you and your needs in friendship. And, you must be receptive to that person's needs.

The person with a positive outlook on life and one who enjoys growth and change savors each of the six levels of friendship.

The newspaperwoman from New Jersey explains it this way: "It's a reciprocal relationship. You can't be friends all by yourself. It's like the tango—it takes two."

What are your needs in such a friendship? What is your definition of a friend? What are some of the qualities you desire in a friend? What are your expectations? Think about that for a moment.

IMPORTANT QUALITIES

The overwhelming first choice of what people want in a friend is: loyalty. "Someone I can trust" is heard over and over again.

Take a look at the list below and see how many of these qualities you consider important in a friend.

1. Loyalty
2. Honesty
3. Respect
4. Intelligence
5. Sincerity
6. Dependability
7. Common interests
8. Understanding
9. Compassion
10. Sense of humor
11. Good listener
12. Sound values and standards

What others would you add? Are any of these important to you?

1. Trustworthiness
2. Consistency
3. Tolerance
4. Wide variety of interests
5. Sharing self and others
6. Warmth and outgoingness
7. Liking self
8. Good conversationalist
9. Discretion (can keep a secret)
10. Enjoyment of doing things together
11. Discussion of ideas in depth
12. Availability when needed

What other considerations are important to you in your friendships? Would you add any of the following?

1. Ethnic background
2. Religious background
3. Educational background
4. Economic level
5. Geographic location
6. Kind of vocation or profession
7. Attractive physical appearance
8. Good family background
9. Member of the right groups
10. Right associates
11. Accomplishment in field of work
12. Eagerness to go places and do things

Make a list for yourself. Use any of the items in these lists that are important to you. Think about the different levels of friendship and then ask yourself, "What qualities are really important to me in a friend?"

Be honest with yourself. No one knows what *you* really like except you. Some people care more about certain things than others. If an attractive physical appearance in a friend is important to you, put it on your list. Maybe you prefer your friends under thirty or over forty. If you're six feet four and you are uncomfortable with anyone under five feet eight, put that on your list. These are important considerations for you. If you like exuberant, outgoing people—that's fine. But if in your heart you really prefer people who are quiet most of the time, and good listeners, put that on your list.

Even when others say, "Jerry's got a great sense of humor, he's always cheerful," you may think, so cheerful, sometimes I'd like to strangle him! *Cheerful* may not be a quality you look for in a friend.

If you're a Phi Beta Kappa who graduated magna cum laude from college, intelligence is an important quality in most of your friendships.

Of course, you realize you won't find all these qualities in any one person. Just as you have many facets to your personality, other people will offer different facets of themselves to you. We all have different friends for different reasons and needs. We enjoy those differences. Some of our friends are outgoing and exuberant, while others are scholarly and withdrawn.

Some friends have only one color, they are entertaining or charming, intelligent or fun-loving, but one quality is so vivid, it is enough. Often that friend encourages a similar quality in you or removes the burden from you to be that way.

SIMILARITIES AND DIFFERENCES

Think about some of the friends you already have or the people you'd like to know better. What do you like about them? Maybe what you like about them is how they affect you.

"I have to be sharp when Sally's around, really on my toes. She's so quick-witted, its a challenge to keep up with her. I love every minute of it. Although . . . I'm not sure I could take it as a steady diet," a young computer programmer confides.

"So-and-so brings out the best in me!" is another line everyone has heard, if not said, at one time or another. Do you know someone who brings out the best in you? Is that a quality you'd like in a friend?

You may discover that the quality you like in one person seems an annoying characteristic in another.

"I don't understand it!" a saleswoman says. "I really admire the way Millie speaks up. She's so outgoing. All the customers like her. She always has something to say to everybody. But when Diane does the same thing, she antagonizes people. She rubs everyone the wrong way—including me!"

You've probably had a similar experience and know that it's not always *what* a person does but the *way* the person does it that counts.

"It ain't what you do, it's the way that you do it," as the old song puts it.

So—there's something more there than the way Millie speaks up. What is there about Millie? Take another look. Could it be that Millie cares about others and Diane doesn't?

Take a look at how Millie handles a customer as compared to Diane:

MILLIE: May I help you?
CUSTOMER: Yes, I'd like to see that blue scarf.
MILLIE: This one here? It is the most beautiful blue, isn't it?
CUSTOMER: Yes, I think so.
MILLIE: Is it for you?
CUSTOMER: Yes.
MILLIE: It matches your pretty blue eyes.
CUSTOMER: Thank you. I'll take it.

DIANE: May I help you?
CUSTOMER: Yes, I'd like to see that blue scarf.
DIANE: Which one? They're all blue this season.
CUSTOMER: (points) That one, there.
DIANE: Everyone wants blue this year.
CUSTOMER: Do they?
DIANE: That's what the fashion magazines say. Don't you read Vogue?
CUSTOMER: Eh . . . I don't know. I think I'll look further, thank you.

The subtle difference here, of course, is that Millie is interested in her customer and what she wants. Diane is more interested in impressing her customer with her own knowledge.

Do you subscribe to that old adage, "You are judged by the company you keep"? If you do, having the right friends is important to you. You may want to proceed more cautiously than someone who doesn't see himself reflected in his choice of friends. Friends offer you a mirror reflection of what you are or what you'd like to be. Adolescent friends mirror each other in dress, action, and even speech.

Some people are concerned with having the "right" friends. They want to be a part of an ingroup. They want to see themselves as being a "right" person. Along with the "right" friends are the "important" friends. The thinking is that the man who has "important" friends is an important man himself.

Maybe you lean more to the other side of the fence which says, "opposites attract."

"I want a friend who's different from me, someone who has qualities I'm missing. That way we complement each other.

"You know, it's like my two daughters when they do the dishes. If they both wanted to wash all the time, there would be constant WAR. But one likes to wash and one likes to dry; there's harmony. They complement each other," says a housewife and mother from Ohio.

If you're like most of us, you're attracted to both types for different reasons, depending on the time and place.

COMMON CHARACTERISTICS

Now, let's examine the kinds of people who are attracted to you. What are some of the characteristics that your friends and acquaintances have in common? These characteristics can be assets or liabilities. Don't pass judgment, just be realistic with the characteristics you list. If you can find some common denominators, you'll have an idea of the kinds of people who are attracted to you. If you are already attracting the people you want for friends, you're way ahead of the game. It's a matter of building the relationship from one level to the next.

Remember Millie, the salesgirl who spoke up? Here's a list of some of the qualities Millie's friends have in common. From this list do you think she's attracting the kind of people she wants for friends?

1. Fun-loving
2. Loud, boisterous
3. Hard-working
4. Enjoys talking
5. Active (goes places and does things)
6. Intelligent

Make your list. What qualities do people share who are attracted to you? Think about each of your friends and acquaintances in relationship to each other. Are they all intellectuals? Athletes? Both? Do they have any other qualities in common?

That's your second list. The first one shows the qualities you look for in a friend. The second shows the qualities your friends and acquaintances share. Any similarities? Perhaps you need to enlarge the areas of your interests to attract the kind of people you want for friends.

No one can be all things to all people, and no wise person would try. Aristotle said, "A friend to all is a friend to none."

One of the universals of friendships is that everybody needs it. Everyone can be a friend and have a friend. There is no scarcity of people. The trick is to find those you want for friends and work toward building and/or strengthening the relationship into a meaningful one of the fifth or sixth level.

Pamela is a lawyer who likes all kinds of people. Although she was an only child, she is anything but an introvert. Why does she have more friends than most people?

Pamela answers this way: "I think an only child begins by looking inside herself for sustenance or outside to others. In my case I looked outside to others for a friend that would be that sister or brother I didn't have. Friends come in all shapes, sizes, colors, and ages. I guess I'm still looking. Oh, I still call my oldest friend— Sis."

You may find a friend who says, "We're as alike as two peas in a pod." Another might say, "You couldn't find two more opposite persons on the face of the earth."

How lucky for you if you enjoy both! "Variety is the spice of life," as they say.

The question most people ask is: "How do I begin? Where do I start? I'm too old to walk up to somebody and say, 'Hey, how would you like to be my friend?'"

You can learn to be friendly. Notice the word—*friendly.* You can be friendly without being a friend. If you are friendly, you will attract people to you. You will operate easily on friendship levels 1 and 2. From there you can decide which of these relationships you want to build into a higher level friendship.

SIGNALS

Send out your own signals that say, "I'm available for friendship."

Cultivate a sincere interest in other people.

Do things with people.

Present an open stance, and an open mind to others.

Offer to help in whatever way you can.

Learn to ask the questions that will help the relationship move to a higher level.

Everyone knows someone like Harry. They all say, "He's a friendly guy." Yet of a person like Calvin, people say, "He's a cold fish." What is it that makes one person that way and another the opposite?

Chances are Harry sends out some kind of signal that says: "I'm friendly and open to others. I like people." And he probably smiles. That's the first characteristic that comes to mind when you say *friendly*. One of the few things psychiatrists agree on is the value of a smile. "In our society the smile is the universal signal, the accepted first step in being friendly." We all like to see it. Just as the song says, "Smile, darn you, smile."

One woman who has her own cosmetics firm has the nickname Frieda Friendly. She laughs when people call her that, but everyone agrees she is friendly.

"She's always smiling and seems to enjoy life. It doesn't matter if she's with old friends or some of those high-powered executives she works with, she's always the same relaxed, open person," a friend describes her.

One of her employees says: "She's easy to be with. You'd never know she runs a multimillion-dollar business. She's not critical except in a helpful way, and she never yells when you make a mistake."

"Frieda makes you feel important. She knows you're there. You know how some people look right through you when they want to see who else is around? Frieda looks at you like you're the only one in the room," adds her accountant.

We can't all be like Frieda, but we can learn to be friendly. How does Frieda do it?

She puts it this way: "I just like people, that's all, so it's easy for me. It's been a great asset in my business. I think there's something to learn from every person I meet. I try to find out what's special about them. I guess that comes across somehow."

She thought for a moment and then went on. "If a person is nervous and uptight, he can't really tell you about himself or his special interest. So I take some time and try to put the other person at ease. Usually, I find something funny and get him laughing. That's the best way I know to relax. I guess other people think so too."

When asked if she had lots of friends, Frieda said: "I'd say, I have lots of *acquaintances* or *companions*, but just two or three good friends. I can be friendly with everyone, but not friends. There just isn't time."

Frieda knows the difference between being friendly and being a friend and uses it to her advantage.

What were some of the traits people mentioned to describe Frieda? Which of these character traits did you notice in the mini-character sketch of Frieda?

1. Smiles a lot
2. Is joyful
3. Has an easy, relaxed manner
4. Is accepting (noncritical)
5. Looks you straight in the eye
6. Cares about people
7. Tries to put others at ease
8. Has a sense of humor
9. Shows interest in others
10. Encourages laughter

Do all these characterize *friendly* to you? What other traits would you add—a warm handshake, a desire to please, an outgoing manner? Any others? Make a list for yourself of the character traits that add up to "friendly." Now take a look at your list. Have you characterized *friendly* in a way that only a politician looking for votes would measure up? Which of these characteristics are important to you in a friend? A word of warning—not everyone responds to the same kind of friendliness. Sometimes just being yourself, at ease, will encourage someone to seek you out.

The lyrics from a children's song put it very simply: "A friend is someone you like, someone who likes you."

NEEDS

What kind of friend do you *want*? Is this the same kind of friend you need? Is there a difference?

Let's look at some of the needs in a friendship. Some people need friends who are located close by. Some need friends with similar ethnic backgrounds, educational level, or work-related jobs, career goals, etc. They need to see and be with their friends daily. They need reinforcement of themselves through their friends.

Most close friendships begin in proximity. If the friendship grows strong enough, it can endure separation. Many such friendships that began in proximity can thrive now with visits only once or twice a year. Lucky the person who has a friend throughout his or her lifetime. Those are rare and special relationships, and take a special kind of nurturing and trust. There must be growth and change on both sides. Yet these friends maintain a special wavelength for each other. That kind of friendship most often reaches the fifth or sixth level.

The Six Levels of Friendship
Let's take another look at the six levels of friendship and expand each somewhat. Most people experience the first two levels with very little difficulty. To achieve the next four takes some concentration and effort. To achieve the last two, and especially the sixth level, takes a very special kind of caring and nurturing and a lot of work on both sides. It takes responsibility on both parts.
Everyone needs:

1. *Someone to talk to* even if it's about the weather, baseball scores, the boss, or a new recipe.
2. *Someone to play or work with.* Adults play lots of games like tennis, golf, baseball, volleyball, Mah-jongg, Scrabble, backgammon, bridge. They work on job projects, for community services, and in neighborhood-related activities.
3. *Someone to count on.* Everyone needs a good neighbor, someone close by to help out when needed.
4. *Someone to share mutual experiences and special times with* whether it's at home, at work, at school, in the community, or in any group-related happenings.
5. *Someone to share thoughts and ideas; life of the mind.* This person is the one you trust as a sounding board for your ideas and your growing.
6. *Someone to trust who will respect and support you and your growth.* This someone will accept you for who you are, and where you are in life, and share hopes, dreams, and disappointments. This person gives complete loyalty and will support you through good times and bad.

Close friendships don't just happen, somebody makes them happen. There are times when a friendship seems one-sided, with one person doing all the caring and sharing. But at another time the pendulum will swing and the other person will be the one who cares and shares. Friendship must be constant. You must be there when your friend needs you. If not in body—in spirit. You can't be a friend one day and not the next.

60

An old friend offered this bit of advice: "Friendship is like a garden. First you select carefully the best plants you can find. Don't bother with any varieties that aren't pleasing to you. Choose the sturdiest ones that will grow well in your soil and fit in with the rest of your garden. Cultivate and care for judiciously and continually!"

CHAPTER 5

Choices:
One Best Friend
or Several Friends

"I'll be your best friend" is the line heard among youngsters when one wants something from the other. That offer of friendship is the prize or reward bid for some desired favor or action. However, it's much easier said than done. This offer is not so freely proffered among adults, and very rarely verbalized when it is.

A manicurist in Philadelphia relates this poignant story from her childhood: "When I was a kid, I thought a best friend had to be yours alone and you had to be hers. I thought it was some kind of special relationship that two persons agreed to and swore a kind of oath to make it happen. I remember asking this girl in my neighborhood if she would be my best friend. I laid out the conditions very carefully and made a list of exactly what I expected in this relationship. There would be no room for anyone else in this rarefied state of being best friends. She turned me down cold! I was devastated."

That story illustrates most graphically that a best friend is rarely picked out in advance, nor is she offered a relationship that doesn't already exist. The *best-friend* relationship evolves through time and shared experiences.

A technical director in New York says this: "I see each friend as a best friend. Each is a best friend for a certain part of him. One person is my best friend for talking. Another is my best friend for doing; and yet another is my best friend for the joy of being. Each of these persons is a best friend to me in one area or another. Actually, I think anyone who can deal with me—as I am—has to be more than an acquaintance. I don't have the time or energy for casual relationships. Each time I have a friendship, that friend is my 'best friend' at that moment. No one person can be a best friend all the time. I prefer to have several different people who function as my 'best friend' at different times in different situations.

"A *real* friend—I like that term better than 'best friend,' anyway—a real friend understands from my perspective. If I think something is good for me, my friend does too. He is in tune with where I am at this point in time. If I see something else that's wrong for me, my friend usually sees it that way too, i.e., a mate, a job, another kind of opportunity. My friend usually thinks like I do about the things that are important to me.

"Of course, situations change, and people change, but my friends seem to care enough about me so that we are on the same wavelength."

The term *best friend* is probably fantasized as often as that other illusive term, *one true love.*

What are the expectations in a close friendship? What do most people expect in a best friend, or true friend (or whatever term you choose for the person who is special in your life at this point in time)?

QUALITIES IN FRIENDS

"I want someone who will believe in me, someone who will see my good qualities . . . or should I say, 'see through to my good qualities' even when I don't know they're there. That person has to be someone I can depend on, or even *lean* on when I need to," explains a therapist in Washington.

A psychiatrist at the same hospital puts it this way: "It's someone to whom you can reveal your vulnerability, and the person won't move in for the kill."

A young career woman named Ruth, when asked to describe her best friend, explains: "We operate on the same wavelength. We know each other so well. That first layer of how you want people to perceive you is peeled away. You let that person see you just as you are. That makes you vulnerable. Trust is so important in the relationship. You trust the other person to listen to your problems and feelings, and you don't feel threatened by exposing yourself like that."

She paused for a moment, searching for the right words to express her feelings. "It's a mutual caring. That's what's so special—the mutuality of the relationship. It's pretty even."

Another young woman offers: "No one person can answer all of my needs. I'm not the same all the time. Sometimes I want someone who is happy, cheerful, and fun. I feel like kicking up my heels and saying: 'I'm glad to be alive! I'm happy for this moment.'

"Then there are other times when everything goes wrong. Things are so bad for me it's all I can do to just be someplace, to sit quietly with someone and not talk—just be. Now, I need two very different people for those two different moods. I sure don't want to put up with Happy Hannah when I feel like Depressing Dora.

"We need different people for different moods—just as we are different people when we are in different moods."

A thirty-nine-year-old journalist prefers several close friends to one best friend. "You can't get everything from one person, so why try," she says. "But I'm lucky, I have three friends I grew up with, and we're still close. So you see I'm three times as lucky as someone who has only one best friend."

"I don't want to depend on any one person for friendship," states a salesman from Chicago. "I like people for different reasons. And I want somebody there when I need him and not when he wants to be there or when it's convenient to be there. I like to do things with people, so for me I need someone who's available, that's all—just someone who's available."

Some people are more comfortable with one person. They find it much easier to relate on a one-to-one basis. Others prefer several people for company. Just as one person prefers swimming or weight lifting by himself, another finds his recreation in team sports.

Don't underestimate the role of circumstances in your friendship preference. If you come in contact with a great many people in your life, you may need just one constant—a best friend. That person whom you can fall back on and say, "I need someone to listen."

If you deal with only a few people during the course of your day, you may want several people to share your relaxing time.

If you decide a best friend is for you, you must be willing to work at the relationship and take the responsibility for that friendship. With responsibility comes acceptance of things that cannot be changed.

One good friend may be all you need. Learn to accept his faults. When things go wrong, don't dwell on the negative aspects. Learn to discuss the unfriendly behavior. If something bothers you, talk about it. Tell your friend it bothers you. Allow your friend the same privilege. Learn to say: "I can see how that bothers you. I'll see what I can do about it."

RESPONSIBILITIES

An intimate relationship with one person demands greater responsibility from both parties. Each is responsible for the other person in some way, and each must take this responsibility seriously. Along with responsibility comes vulnerability. If you accept the responsibility for another person, you in turn become vulnerable to that person and/or criticism about that person. When you become vulnerable, you are open to the wounds and hurts the other person may inflict on you, intentionally or unintentionally. You are vulnerable to his pain as well as your own.

Most people don't suddenly decide they want a best friend, nor do they pick one out. The relationship occurs through a series of interrelated experiences over a period of time.

An old friend named Georgia explains it this way: "Friendship is based on the original cementing of two people at a vital, growing period in one's life—which often synthesizes the core of that particular friendship, i.e., in school years, career, parenthood."

If you decide a best friend is the relationship you want, proceed slowly and build the relationship step by step. Remember the manicurist's childhood story of asking another youngster to be her best friend. Don't make the mistake the manicurist did. You may be in for a disappointment.

There is responsibility in every friendship but always a greater one in a close relationship. Some people do not want that responsibility.

It is much easier to be ONE in this life, unencumbered by family or friends. With a relationship comes a responsibility. Be sure you are willing to assume the responsibility of a special friendship. You may decide you prefer your relationships on a more limited basis with little or no responsibility involved.

Each person makes an individual choice. People who are not willing to accept the responsibility are much happier with a group of people. The responsibility in these relationships is much less. Social groups, fraternal groups, etc., are perfect examples of this kind of relationship. Everybody has someone and yet no one is responsible for anyone else. The group is responsible for everyone.

PROS AND CONS

Many people are better off with several friends than with a best friend. There are pros and cons for each. Only you can decide which is the best kind of relationship for you.

Some people choose one best friend because that person:

believes in you
is dependable
understands you
accepts you
trusts you and you trust
cares about you
shares your interests
is comfortable to be with
is sensitive to your needs
is responsible to you and for you
cherishes your vulnerability
listens
is accessible to you
encourages your growth

Some people prefer to have several friends because those persons offer:

a wide variety of interests
diverse opinions
availability
growth in many directions
acceptance of you on your terms
no responsibility
no demands on you or your time
conversation on many subjects
good listeners
persons there when you need them
diverse life-styles
no emotional involvement

"I don't ever remember having a *best* friend. I never had *one* person. I always had best friends. These friends were equal in my eyes," states a forty-five-year-old director. "These best friends were my friends for different reasons. One friend has a great sense of humor. He loves to read and write. We correspond regularly now. Another friend was big and strong physically. I felt safe with him. The third was a fellow artist who wanted and shared the same kind of artistic goals. The same type of plays interested both of us. He was a brother in the arts."

66

How can you tell which is best for you: one best friend or several friends? Are some people just naturally more inclined to one kind of friendship than others?

Many people find it very difficult to confide in anyone, let alone more than one person. For that person anything other than one friend would be out of the question.

For people who are not often in the same place to cultivate the same friends, building a support network of several friends is important.

Examine your own needs and preferences. Do you usually find one friend to whom you confide or do you function best with several different people? Perhaps you haven't thought about it before. Find out for yourself which is better for you: a best friend or several friends.

Answer the ten questions below with YES, NO, or SOME-TIMES.

TEST: ARE YOU BEST SUITED FOR ONE BEST FRIEND OR SEVERAL FRIENDS?

1. Do you like to play games alone or with a partner, better than as part of a team?
2. Do you enjoy meeting all kinds of people and going to new places?
3. Are your friends usually similar to you?
4. Do you like the feeling of responsibility for others as well as for yourself?
5. Are you willing to go out of your way to do a favor for someone, even when you have other things to do?
6. Do you prefer to plan things for yourself and others rather than go along with others' plans?
7. Do you like to share your inner feelings and thoughts with others?
8. Can you accept the faults of others without getting annoyed?
9. Do you like to go when and where you choose and have the feeling of independence?
10. Do you like people to know you well enough to be sensitive to your needs without your telling them?

If you answered YES to questions 1, 3, 4, 5, 7, 8, and 10, you probably prefer to have a best friend.

If you answered NO to questions 1, 4, and 10 and YES to questions 2, 6, 9, you're probably best suited to have several friends rather than one best friend.

One of the problems we all face in a friendship is accepting the faults of others. We all want our friend to be perfect. Many people see others as they want them to be, not as they are.

We create elaborate scenarios in our minds of how our friend will act and what he will say. When this scene is played out not the way we imagined it, we are disappointed. All too often we are disappointed in our friend.

The earliest collection of English colloquial sayings tells us, "There are none so blind as those that will not see." Learn to accept a friend as he is, not as you wish him to be. No one person can survive being placed on a pedestal. Take another look. Concentrate on the real qualities that attract you to that person. What are the qualities he offers that nurture the relationship? Emphasize those attributes and learn to accept the faults. Make a list for yourself. See how many more qualities than faults you can list. That will show you how many more good points than bad your friend has to offer.

The responsibility in friendship can weigh heavily at times, especially if your loyalty is tested by more than one friend at a time.

"Three of my friends decided to have nervous breakdowns at the same time," exclaims a thirty-eight-year-old woman named Connie. "By noon yesterday I was an emotional cripple." And with a grimace she added, "Who needs friends?"

Although the last sentence was said in jest, this woman had to face the all-too-common problem of conflicting loyalties among her friends.

What are you to do when two friends each invite you to something they consider very important? Obviously, a choice must be made; the manner of acceptance and rejection must be carefully worked out. In a case like this, your own wishes should guide the decision. Which invitation do you want to accept? If you value honesty in a relationship, you must be prepared to use it. The honesty you must bring to each relationship is important, as well as the honesty to yourself.

"This above all: to thine own self be true," Shakespeare wrote.

But what if you truly can't decide what you would rather do? When in doubt fall back on the old first-come, first-served basis. What's fair? Of course, there are complications there too. What if one person assumed you were going someplace with him or her because you do every year, and the other person asked you first this year? A dilemma, but not unlike many such dilemmas in friendship. Consider the two parties involved. Is one of them better eqiupped to handle the rejection than the other? Is one more understanding than the other? Is one more mature?

Sometimes your only solution is not to accept either invitation. Stay home or go someplace else by yourself. A family or medical commitment is always an accepted out if you need an excuse. Every friend will understand. And if your friend doesn't understand, perhaps this friend is too demanding of your time, and you need to introduce more space and/or distance in your relationship.

CHANGING NEEDS

Along with the problem of conflicting loyalties in friendship is the problem of the changing needs and goals in one person or the other. For example, what do these people have in common now?

JANE: Well, if it isn't . . . Mary! Right? Mary T. Justin, my best friend in junior high school.

MARY: Why, it's Jane! Jane, . . . dear Jane, how are you?

JANE: Oh, I'm just fine, and you?

MARY: Fine! Fine! I'm a college professor now—just like I always said I would be.

JANE: Oh!

MARY: And what about you? Did you become a great actress? Are you an actress, like you always said you would be?

JANE: Well, no, not really. You must have gone back to school to become a professor.

MARY: Oh, I did. I sure did. I took my M.A. twenty years after my B.A. It was hard. Then the doctorate.

JANE: You always got good grades.

MARY: It was different in grad school. You had to think. I thought of you a lot then and those crazy late-night discussions we used to have.

JANE: Oh.

MARY: Yes, you really made me think about a lot of things.

JANE: I did?

MARY: Sure, don't you remember all that stuff we used to talk about? How we were going to change the world and make it a better place for everyone to live in.

JANE: Oh, yeah, I guess. We were so young.

MARY: But tell me about you. What are you doing?

69

JANE: Not much.

MARY: How's . . . oh, what's his name?

JANE: Howie.

MARY: Yeah, Howie. You were so crazy about him. He was the most important thing in your life then, even more so than the career. Whatever happened to Howie?

JANE: I married him.

MARY: Oh, how is he?

JANE: Fine, I guess. I haven't seen him in the past three years. We're divorced.

MARY: Oh!

JACK: Hey, you old son of a gun, what are you doing here?

TOM: I told you I wouldn't miss our twentieth class reunion.

JACK: But you were in Europe. Don't tell me you came back just for this?

TOM: Not exactly. I thought as long as I was going to be here, I'd catch your daughter's wedding.

JACK: You old so-and-so, why didn't you say that in the first place?

TOM: Anybody who keeps in touch with me for twenty years deserves me to be at his daughter's wedding—not to mention the greatest wedding present I could find.

DICK: It's been twenty years. How are you?

CHARLOTTE: Fine, just fine. I'm still in the restaurant business.

DICK: I know. So am I.

CHARLOTTE: You are?

DICK: Sure. When I moved to Seattle from here, I remembered everything you taught me about supply and demand. They needed a restaurant just like the one you had back in Cincinnati.

CHARLOTTE: Well, aren't you something. Tell me all about it.

DICK: Well, I started in a small way, just like you did here in Cincinnati, and I . . .

As you can tell, the last dialogues show a relationship that can pick up where it left off. The first one may be a problem.

Your best friend ten years ago may be merely an acquaintance today. People grow in different directions. Sometimes growth

70

occurs at the same time. More often it does not. Circumstances beyond our control affect relationships.

Be prepared to accept change in a relationship. Take pleasure in what you have. Enjoy the time you function on the same wavelength, the flow of energy back and forth. Realize that there are times in a friendship when one person gives more than the other.

Accept your needs for time to grow. One old friend sums it up this way: "Understand the changes in yourself and respect them in others. Your relationship is not the same as it was once. Don't live in the past." She paused thoughtfully. "And don't be angry if the other person doesn't change."

We all adapt to life's situations in our own way. The book *Adaptation to Life,* which gives the results of the Grant study of Harvard graduates, showed that man's adaptive devices are as important in determining the course of his life as his heredity, his upbringing, his social position, or his access to psychiatric help.

With the mobility of today's world, many old friends go their separate ways. Sometimes you stay on the same wavelength, so that your hookups are easily restored when you come back together. Your inner self is still immediately accessible to the other person. Here's what several people say about their friend in common, Harry:

> "Old Harry, he's a brick. He'll never change. He's my friend."
> "Harry's not the same person he used to be, but he's still my friend."
> "Harry is the one constant in life. It's great for me, but I'm not so sure how good it is for Harry."
> "Harry, good old Harry, always changing. He's my best friend—always has been—always will be."

Harry has changed more to some of his friends than others. I wonder what Harry might say about each of his friends who commented above.

In order for friendship to endure through various growth levels, there must be communication and a sensitivity to each other's needs. With these elements present, friendship will survive and become an enduring relationship, space and time notwithstanding.

It's a feeling of playing on the same team.

When you have one person you know will always catch the pass you throw, you throw with confidence. When you know you have blocking from several people when you carry the ball, you will run with confidence and carry the ball all the way for a touchdown. It's a question of style. Which style do you choose at this point in time? Your style today may not be the style you choose for tomorrow.

Isn't it wonderful you have a choice?

CHAPTER 6

Bridging the Gap
from Acquaintance to Friend

"Cross over the bridge," advises an old gospel song.

These words, of course, are symbolic; they mean the linking together of two separate states. Those states can be of grace, geographic location, or the mind. Take your choice. Whichever image you choose, the instructions are clear. In order to cross over, from any one place to another, you must take action and frequently a risk as well.

It is the same when you bridge the gap from acquaintance to friend. You must take action. How can you take this action with the least risk? There is always risk involved when you reach out to another person. The risk is rejection. That rejection is harmful to the ego and the whole sense of self.

If I am a worthwhile human being, others will perceive me like that; hence they will accept my offer of friendship. Conversely, when that offer of friendship is rejected, the cause-to-effect rationale says, "You refused my offer of friendship; hence, I am not a worthwhile human being."

As we grow older, the risk gets harder to take.

Young children find friends as easily as they find a place to play. They do things together: play, build, run, slide. Very often even talk is unnecessary. Sometimes laughter comes before talk. Frequently, the joy of doing erupts in gleeful laughter.

SIMPLE BEGINNINGS

There's something to be learned from the simplicity of children's friendships. Do something together. Work together, play together. Share an interest. Start a project. Take a genuine interest in what the other person is doing. Go out of your way to help that person or do a favor—and you begin to make a friend.

Young children have little experience in selection in their friendships. The only important element is to be at the same place and accept the other's presence there. Young children make their connections easily and uninhibitedly. There is something refreshing about watching children play. The flexibility of the games, the needs, what the environment can be, all offer little in the way of problems. There is a beautiful immediacy about play.

An artist says: "What keeps me fresh, my work . . . alive and new, is my ability never to lose the child in me. I cherish my playfulness. I cherish my heart of the child. If I ever lose that, I think I shall cease to be an artist."

Children play as easily as they eat and breathe. The imagination can bridge any gap that exists. They have learned very few taboos about whom to play with and what to play.

Furthermore, their friendships are immediate—if also temporary. The ritualistic steps of moving through to a relationship are expurgated. Very few adults can begin an acquaintance as easily as a child can. On the other hand, some adults find friendships easier to come by now than when they were young.

"It's easier to make friends now than it was when I was younger," observes a doctor in Philadelphia. "Competition in my life is starting to disappear. Young people today are more concerned with security than with competition. Their demands on life are less, so they have more time to devote to friends."

Then what are the signs that signal when a relationship is ready for a change? Certain ingredients must be ready to be added or already in place. What are the essential ingredients that signal a change in the level of a relationship?

Reciprocity is one such ingredient. Don't expect what you are not willing to give. When you discover you are willing to give more than you have heretofore, that person could be a friend. It works in both directions. Be aware when the other person is reaching out, when you see him offering to give more than he has in the past. Both of these signs give strong signals to the individuals in a relationship.

Samuel Johnson offers this observation on friendship: "Friendship is seldom lasting, but between equals."

An old Persian proverb looks at the relationship from the opposite side: "Friendship with a fool is like the embrace of a bear."

PROMOTING FRIENDSHIP

In brief, what are the outside elements that promote friendship?

Proximity, of course, is number one. Shared interests is a close second.

"A similar outlook on life is most important to me. That's what ignites my friendship," admits a dental technician in Michigan. "When you have a similar outlook on life with someone, you can be sure you have some similar goals also. You know you have a common meeting ground."

Her twenty-two-year-old assistant says: "I think having fun together is what promotes my friendship. You don't have to know a person's life goals or outlook on life for that. If something is fun for both of you, that's what counts. And that makes friends."

Having fun together can cover a diverse spectrum of activities. Perhaps there is nothing that promotes a happy time more than laughter does. When you find the same things funny or laugh at a similar situation, you're usually on the same wavelength. If you both laugh at yourself, you have something in common.

Many people prefer an active association, doing something together. A well-known bridge player remarks, "I can tell more about the way a man thinks by playing cards with him than I can in a week-long discussion about common goals and life values." He adds, "I guess you could say playing cards is my way of having fun."

"What prompts my friendship is a sense of humor about life situations. That's my common denominator. When I find someone who laughs at the same things I do, I know that person could be my friend." This from a lighting designer in New York. "Of course, if that person is cheerful, happy, optimistic, and fun to be with, then I know we're basically alike and have a lot in common," he added. with a smile.

In addition to proximity and shared interests as elements that promote friendship, add similar goals, having fun together, and the same sense of humor.

RESPECTING A FRIEND

"Mutual respect is important," offers a thirty-three-year-old commercial artist. "When you show regard or someone shows regard for your well-being, you know respect is there."

Indeed, *respect* is a word that bears close examination. Respect implies "esteem, courtesy, and consideration." We all show respect for many people we've never met: the President, the pope, the mayor of our city.

Respect, then, would seem vital in promoting friendship. You would not intrude on someone you respected. Courtesy to that person would also be a sign of respect.

Is respect a *given* or must it be *earned?* Do you respect everyone? After all, the world would be a better place if everyone respected everyone else. However, in reality, respect seems to be a quality that must be brought about on the basis of some evidence. Therefore, respect is an important ingredient to promote friendship.

On the other hand, one of the best ways to promote friendship is to show a sincere interest in the other person. Show interest in his hopes and dreams as well. Along with that sincere interest, be prepared to take action on his behalf if necessary. A friend would be willing to drop what he's doing if his help is needed.

"I want a friend I can call at 3:00 A.M. with a terrible problem and she won't hang up on me. And she'll really care about my problem," says a fund raiser in New York.

Another way to show your interest in another person is to learn to ask the right questions.

ASKING QUESTIONS

How are you? How are you really? What are you feeling? What are you thinking? What do you care about? What are your concerns at this moment? How do you feel about this, that, and the other thing? What's happening deep-down inside you?

If the answer is, "I never thought about that before," then you have widened the universe, even if just a little, for that person.

"I don't like to intrude on other people's privacy," admits a thirty-nine-year-old history teacher. "I don't ask enough questions—or questions on the right subjects."

What the teacher needs to learn is to ask the kinds of questions that will allow the other person to share himself. Not everyone can begin with the in-depth questions above. But everyone can ask simple nonthreatening questions that don't ask for self-disclosure. People who become friends want to talk about what is important to them.

Start with simple, direct questions like: How do you feel about that? What do you think of . . . ? What would you do? What should I do about . . . ?

Get her opinion. Ask for advice. Let her know that her thoughts are valuable to you. These are the kinds of questions that prompt sharing of feelings. And listen to her answers, really listen. You can reinforce your own listening as well as let the other person know you're listening by such comments as: "What you mean is . . . , right?" or "I'm not sure I understand what you mean by that. Would you say it again?"

Good talk is like good wine; it's to be savored. While you have it, enjoy it. Remember it for its excellent flavor and body. Cherish it so that you will want it the next time.

BRIDGING THE GAP

It takes time and effort. Each person must find her own way to help it grow. She must reinforce the connection to help bridge the gap from acquaintance to friend.

Remember, friendship can't be rushed. People must find their own opportunity for it to happen. Bridging the gap takes time and energy.

Moreover, the person must ask himself if he really wants to push this relationship to the next level. If he is content with the relationship where it is, there is no reason to spend the time and effort necessary for bridging the gap.

On the other hand, if the person is truly bent on promoting the relationship to the friendship category, here are the specific ways to work at it. Read them carefully and let your mind digest their message.

TEN WAYS TO BRIDGE THE GAP
FROM ACQUAINTANCE TO FRIEND

1. Seek out the other person's company.
2. Participate in an activity together.
3. Share new experiences for both of you.
4. Discover the other's interests, likes and dislikes.
5. Explore those interests plus goals and life values.
6. Listen wholeheartedly.
7. Promote laughter and joyful situations.
8. Respect the other person.

9. Demonstrate your loyalty.
10. Offer support, not judgment.

Not everyone wants or needs the acquaintance to become a friend. Certainly no one wants all his acquaintances to become his friends.

However, with age comes selectivity. "As you get older it's no big scramble for friends," a fifty-year-old man admits. "I reach out sometimes—with a handshake and a smile. If the other person is genuinely interesting and interested, I try to be too.

"At my stage in life, I have very little time for new friends. And I'm a little sad about it. When I meet someone I know I'd like if I could be with them, I know I'm missing something. But I can't help it. There are only twenty-four hours in a day."

Give of yourself. Be there for the other person.

After all, acquaintances are necessary. Many people prefer to keep their relationships in that category. The responsibility to an acquaintance is far less than to a friend. Some people feel that they can use an acquaintance for their own benefit, but would not use a friend in the same way. Acquaintances take far less cultivating and care than friends. There is a great deal to be said for having a variety of people among your acquaintances. For example, your opportunities for learning from people are increased. The more people you know the more you can learn about them and their world.

"Actually, I prefer some of my acquaintances to some of my friends," a thirty-five-year-old secretary says. "Because they are survivors. I like survivors, those people who have an instinct for survival. My test for people I want to spend time with is this, 'Would I take them on a desert island with me?' "

One acquaintance says to his colleague, "When the ship goes down, I want to stand next to you, because you're a survivor."

The survivor test is an example of selectivity at work. Another example of the selection process is offered by a Delaware housewife. She puts it this way: "You have to find friends. They don't come to you. Be friendly even if it's only on the surface. That's how you attract people to you. They you decide which person you want for a friend."

On the other hand, a teacher from Nebraska cautions about getting too involved. "Sometimes you get so busy with acquaintances, you forget your friends."

SHARING YOURSELF

Learn to share yourself. We all have priorities in friendship. We share as much or as little as we choose and/or know how. Learning to share yourself with others comes more easily to those who practice. Here are some simple ways you can learn to share yourself with others.

1. *Be yourself.* When you care for someone, you don't have to be just like him. Remember he liked you and/or was attracted to you for the person you are.

2. *Accept help.* Sometimes sharing is allowing someone else to help you. You admit you are vulnerable when you ask for help. Vulnerability is a very human and appealing quality.

3. *Be sensitive.* Tune in to the other person's needs. Be there for him when he wants or needs you. Try to be aware of how much your presence is needed. Avoid intruding.

4. *Speak up.* Let the other person know how you feel about things. And when you do, don't be afraid to admit you're wrong. Maybe you hated George on sight, but when you got to know him, you realized how wrong you were.

5. *Do things.* Don't always do the things you want to do. Let your friend make the suggestion and follow that at times. Try something new for both of you. Explore adventure in a positive way. Sometimes we respond to the situation rather than the person. Don't bring childhood perceptions with you.

6. *Respond.* Give some kind of feedback. Let the other person know you are aware of his needs whether you are able to meet them or not.

7. *Share silence.* A shared silence between two persons can sometimes be more meaningful than an hour's conversation. It is something to try.

8. *Reciprocate.* Share in as many different ways as you can. Plan things for other people. Arrange a surprise.

9. *Accept others.* Learn to accept the bad traits as well as the good. No two persons are exactly alike. Make the effort to understand the other person. Deal with your differences. Bring them out in the open.

10. *Develop resources.* Help your friends develop their resources as well as yours. Exercise both. Stretch them. Promote independence and self-reliance.

11. *Try new things.* Experiment. Have the courage and confidence to try new things, new experiences, new challenges. Find new ways to grow.

12. *Be honest.* Let your friend know when something doesn't please you or you don't want to do something. Don't play polite. Be honest but don't hurt the other person.

Each friendship is unique. There is something to learn from each one. You are responsible for your choice of friends. You make the decision to bridge the gap from acquaintance to friend. Know when you want to devote the time and energy to build the relationship on another level.

Friendship, like love, is impossible to measure, because the more you give, the more you have to give.

Remember, get to know the child in yourself. Here is a part of you that knows when to make demands on you and when to make demands on others. Assign yourself the responsibility of your relationships.

You can have as many acquaintances or friends as you choose. There's no limit on the supply. But friendship doesn't just happen, someone makes it happen. Be that someone.

CHAPTER 7

Attracting the Kind of Friends You Want

When all is said and done, *you* are the single most important source of friendship in your life. You are responsible for your choice of friends. It's as simple as that.

Why don't you walk up to someone who appeals to you and say, "Hey, you're someone I'd like to know," or "I'll bet you and I could be friends"? Why not? Who's stopping you? The only person stopping you is yourself. What's the worst thing that could happen? Rejection!

Of course, it's easier said than done. Especially if this kind of behavior is not *you*—not your style. Perhaps you can't be quite this obvious, but you can learn to take the initiative in certain ways at certain times. Yet, it is important to be yourself.

"If I came on with a line like that—'You're someone I'd like to know'—it would make me look like the hearty hail-fellow-well-met. And, I'm anything but that. When I have to meet new people in any situation, it's really hard for me," admits Harold, a twenty-six-year-old accountant. "How can I be myself and still take the initiative?"

Harold's question is a valid one, of course. How can he be himself and still make an effort to promote friendship?

The first thing a shy person like Harold needs to realize is there are a lot of other shy people out there too. In fact, there's always somebody a-little-more-so anything—shy, fat, thin, awkward, etc. If Harold can learn to look at the other person and try to put him at ease with a simple, nonthreatening opening line, such as:

"Hi, my name is Harold. What's yours?"
"Do you come here often?"
"Do you have the time?"

"Are you a friend of the host or hostess (or any other name)?"
"What do you think of this place?"
"Do you like this kind of music?"
"Who's your favorite musical group?"
"Read any good books (seen any good films) lately?"

Nothing difficult or threatening about any of these lines, is there? They are small talk. As we discussed before, another term is easy talk. Harold could begin a conversation almost anyplace with one of those sentences and still be himself.

TAKING THE INITIATIVE

Yet there are times in our lives when we must take the initiative if we want to attract friends. Those times aren't always easy.

For example, when we move to a new town or neighborhood, go away to college, take a new job, or spend time in a new place, it's difficult. These kinds of new situations bring us in contact with a whole new set of people. In our grandparents' day many folk lived their whole lives in one place doing one job. They never had to learn to cope with new friends. They had their support systems, their family, their neighborhood, their church, their job, etc. But in today's society, with its greater mobility, many of us must make this adjustment not once but several times. These life changes force us to reach out for new friends.

The more interests you have, the more people you can talk to. The wider variety of associations you have, the greater your choice for friends.

What are some things you like to do? Make a list of the ten activities you like most. Rank them in order of your preference.

For example, one list may look like this:

FAVORITE ACTIVITIES

1. Go out to dinner
2. Go to the theatre
3. Walk
4. Swim
5. Read
6. Listen to music
7. Travel
8. Go to parties

9. Dance
10. Play games

Ask a friend to do the same thing; make a list of ten things he or she likes to do in order of preference.

Ideally your friend or friend-to-be will list most of the same activities you did and rank them in the same general order of preference.

On the other hand, an engineer named Jerry, who works as a troubleshooter for his firm in Minneapolis, travels all over the country and sometimes the world. He spends anywhere from two weeks to twenty months in different locations. Luckily he's a friendly guy, so he never wants for companions.

"Most of the people I meet in my work already have a common interest with me," Jerry says, "so the initial step of having something to talk about is no problem. What I do in a new place is just let my interests lead me. I like to go to museums, concerts, the theatre, that kind of thing. I don't go for the usual macho man stuff. So whenever I'm in a new town, I find out what it has to offer in the way of my interests. I enjoy going to those events with or without someone else. I'd rather go to a concert alone than go to a fight with any six people I know. When I meet someone I think I'd like to know better, I make my interests known." He paused for a second and then added: "If those interests turn people off, that's all right too. But I let people know what I like from the beginning. I guess I have learned to be myself and let my interests lead me. It works fine for me!"

On the opposite end of the stick is Marie:

"My husband has changed jobs so many times I can't count anymore," says a twenty-five-year-old housewife named Marie. "And without kids to run interference at the park or playground, it's awfully hard for me to meet women my own age. I'm on my own every time we go to a new place."

Marie has a problem each time she moves. Although she is the traditional housewife, she doesn't have the traditional support systems: no family or relatives nearby and no children to act as instant icebreakers. Her neighbors are new with each move. Marie has only one friend who remains constant—her husband. Still, Marie is able to cope with each situation. How does she do it?

Here's what she says: "My sense of humor helps a lot. I don't let myself get bogged down by self-pity. Whenever I start that, I give

83

myself a mental kick in the pants and say: 'Hey, spend your energy on being the person you want to be. Go *do* something.' And I *do*."

Marie has several active interests. She plays tennis, swims, and thinks nothing of going to the local tennis club to pick up a game with whoever happens to need a partner.

Marie perceives herself as a worthwhile human being, and she is willing to take the risk of rejection if someone else does not perceive her that way. "Heck, I figure anyone with good sense will like me . . . or at least play tennis with me," she says with a smile.

She's had enough success with her mode of operation that she expects a positive outcome from the risks she takes. When that feedback has been positive most of the time, it's easier to take risks.

Consequently, those who are willing to risk have the least to risk.

"I'm interested in all people," says Betty, a recent college graduate. "You can care about so many different kinds. I think I have the opposite problem from most people. With me, I have to keep a lid on my enthusiasm."

Betty had to learn how to direct that friendliness, to be outgoing without being offensive. "If you come on too strong, no matter how sincere you are, you scare people away," she says. "Hey, I was like those little kids who say, 'I'll be your best friend.' "

Betty never liked being alone or doing things alone, so she reached out indiscriminately to anyone who was there. Her perception of herself was of someone who was nothing without someone else with her. When she thought about it, she said: "I was so anxious to please the other person that I was projecting a false image of myself. It wasn't me at all. I never said what I really thought. I was hiding behind a mask. I mean, I was walking around wearing a false face—and it wasn't even Halloween. But now, I like myself better, I can be myself."

Therefore, keep in mind some controls. Be wary of overwhelming new associates and acquaintances. Share slowly as the occasion arises. Recognize the common interests between you and your friend-to-be. Explore those areas slowly and carefully.

Similarly, an older friend of Betty's gave her this advice: "When I meet somebody who could be a potential friend, I say to myself, 'Hey, that person could be my friend.' But I have learned over the years to be cautious about that feeling. I know that if it happens, it happens. In the meantime I will enjoy the relationship—NOW. I have become very selective in my advancing years."

PERCEIVING SELF

Ask yourself this question: Do you perceive yourself as a friend or as the recipient of friendship?

In building a friendship we need to know how people perceive themselves. We have all met the positively beautiful woman who perceives herself as ugly, or the pencil-thin model who won't set foot outside without a girdle because she thinks of herself as being fat.

Our perceptions work the other way too. There's the man who perceives himself as the open, fair-minded parent, as long as his child says what he, the parent, wants to hear. Then there's the woman who thinks of herself as being warm and friendly because she greets everyone she knows with "Darling—Honey—Sweet-heart—Dear."

Many of the perceptions we have of ourselves were established in our childhood. These perceptions can work for or against us. Consequently, the way you perceive yourself can be more important than the way others perceive you. If you perceive yourself as a happy, mature, whole person, chances are you are comfortable with yourself and will have the kind of friends you want.

What is your perception of yourself? Do you have a positive or negative perception?

Try the old line, "Tell me about yourself," to get a friend's perception of how he feels about himself.

Check this rating profile. On a scale from 1 to 10 rate your perception of the following qualities in yourself—10 being the highest and 1 the lowest.

physically attractive	_____
intelligent	_____
humorous	_____
witty	_____
good conversationalist	_____
good company	_____
understanding	_____
patient	_____
honest	_____

good sport	_____
creative	_____
happy	_____
sensitive	_____
sympathetic	_____
tolerant	_____
loyal	_____
dependable	_____
fun-loving	_____
responsible	_____
good listener	_____

Add up your score. How did you rate? Score yourself from 1 to 10 points for each answer on the test.

If you gave yourself 120 points or more total, you have a positive perception of yourself. If you are below that number, find out what your negative perceptions are and where they came from.

If you scored below 120, maybe you should stop for a moment. Look in a large mirror. Ask yourself, "What do I see?" Answer that reflection with the answer of what you see there. And, while you're at it, tell it what you see inside the person as well as on the outside.

RECEIVING FRIENDSHIP

Still, some people find it easier to receive friendship than to give it. They can accept the outstretched hand but cannot offer their own. They can answer the question, "What is your name?" or "How are you?" or "Do you come here often?" But they cannot *ask* the same simple questions of someone else. They can reciprocate (and that's wonderful), but they cannot initiate. They can accept an invitation gladly, but they cannot issue one.

"Of all the things which wisdom provides to make life entirely happy, much the greatest is the possession of friendship." (Epicurus.)

For example, an attractive redhead who works for a publisher says: "I very seldom choose my friends, they choose me. I'm not outgoing or affectionate. I am always the underachiever, so I make others feel superior." She paused for a moment, searching for the right word. "I'm nonthreatening, or noncompetitive."

This woman understands her own ability, however. She knows how to receive friendship when it is offered, even though she cannot instigate it for herself. She is far safer in her role of recipient than she would be as instigator. She knows how to read the signals the other person sends. When the signal says, "I would like you as a friend," she reacts positively to that signal and accepts the other person.

On the other hand, the receiver in a friendship takes a safer road. He has no fear of rejection. He always stays firmly in the driver's seat, in the position of receiving or—rejecting.

For example, a middle-aged man named Jim puts it this way: "It's better to receive than to give. Let the other person take the risk. I don't care what anybody else says. It's much safer for the ego when you let someone else take the first step. And, besides, it's very flattering to be asked to be someone's friend. Oh, not in those words, of course. But that's what the signals tell you."

Then Jim went on to explain the *no risk* involved in accepting or receiving friendship. "I'm not interested in reaching out. I only have time for people who make the first gesture, who reach out for me first." He paused as if surprised at what he had said. "I seldom *seek*, but I will *find* when someone reaches out."

These people talk about responding, but what are some of the skills they use to respond?

Jim stresses, "Read the signals people send you." He then went on to talk about what he calls "the openers." He mentioned the firm handshake, the eye contact, and the interest. "Watch for the sincere smile. Make sure that person surveying the room is not checking to see who else is there and whether there's someone he should talk to. If that person seems genuinely interested and sticks around to talk, respects your opinion, and seems to value the conversation, that tells you something."

Jim thought for a moment before he added: "I respond to that. One thing I've learned is to be perfectly honest with the opinions I express. I let the other person know who I am and what I am. Then if he reaches out, I know he likes the real me."

Jim continued: "When someone seeks you out, spends time with you, and respects your opinions, you know he's interested in you as a person. I'm an open person and I pick up the overture when another person makes it. If it's someone I think I'd like for a friend,

I respond. If not, I let the moment pass. That way it's my choice, you see."

Another person says, "My signal is more of a feeling than an intellectual understanding." The attractive redhead stops to explain. "It's more like a flow of energy back and forth. We are in tune. The sense of humor is most important to me. Do we laugh at the same things; find humor in the same life situations?"

"Also, I think being receptive is a two-way street. One person can't be open or receptive if the other person closes up," another woman offers.

Another acknowledged "receiver" from Ohio put it this way: "I'm quick to pick up on semi-invitations like, 'Let's have lunch sometime.' I show my enthusiasm for the idea."

She went on to say that she gives as many encouraging signals as she can. She smiles, laughs (when it's appropriate), and looks directly at the other person. "I guess I send out vibes that say, 'Please ask, because I like your company.'"

She thought for a moment and then added: "I also go to the places where I think my kind of people will be. I don't really like discos or singles bars." She chuckled at the thought and then added: "Actually, libraries or Great Books groups are more my speed. You know the old adage about 'thieves hang around thieves,' Well, I hang around bookstores or museums."

Nobody can argue with the fact that finding a friend sometimes is just plain luck. You have to be at the right place at the right time. There are many occasions when it is not clear whether another person is reaching out. At those times, encouragement is necessary. Indeed, most of us switch roles from time to time. At one point in our lives we are the instigator; at other points, the receiver. Some people are comfortable with both roles, while others prefer one or the other, and always operate within that one.

YOUR ROLE

Which role do you prefer? Would you rather be the instigator in a friendship or the receiver? Think about that question for a moment and then answer the following with YES or NO:

1. Do you wait for other people to speak to you first?
2. Do you enjoy large parties and socializing with people?
3. Do you consider yourself outgoing and affectionate?
4. Are you afraid of rejection from others?

5. Do you consider it flattering to be selected as a friend?
6. Do you like to invite people to do things with you?
7. Do you express your opinions and ideas openly to others?
8. Do you like to make things happen?
9. Did you ever have a friend you didn't want?
10. Could you walk up to a stranger and say, "You look like someone I'd like to know"?

If your answers to questions 2, 3, 6, 7, 8, and 10 were NO, you are probably more comfortable in the role of receiver. If you answered YES to questions 2, 3, 6, 7, 8, and NO to 4 and 9, the chances are you are more comfortable in the role of instigator.

HOW PATTERNS WORK

Some patterns serve us well throughout our lifetime. Others we would change. Once certain barriers are withdrawn, whole new worlds can open for us. Too many people never stop to look at the patterns or barriers in their lives. They never know whether these patterns help or hinder their development as a whole person at this point in time. A lot of people keep on doing old things in old ways out of habit rather than choice. Habits die hard.

There are times when we'd like to attract the person we admire for a friend. But our old patterns will not allow us to behave in a way that would attract that person. We continue the patterns of our bad habits because we are more comfortable with them. One thing people need most is a feeling of living in a world they understand. In order to change the patterns that restrict us, we must first understand those patterns.

For example, Julia is a thirty-three-year-old advertising copywriter. She is very successful in her job, but not so successful with her choice of friends. "It's always the same person I'm attracted to, the one who takes advantage of me, the one who picks my brain and uses it for his own gain. It's the same whether it's a man or a woman."

She shook her head at her own realization. "That's not as bad as the pattern I see in myself. I keep finding those kinds of people, and I keep going back to the places where I meet them: discos, singles bars, clubs. It's self-destructive. Why can't I wise up?"

Julia has a problem, and although she sees it, she's not willing to take the action necessary to break the pattern. She's comfortable in the environment she knows, even though she knows it's self-destructive. She doesn't really want a change badly enough to do something about it.

On the other hand, Roger has the opposite problem. "I go to places where I find people who like the same things I do: adult education courses, community groups, the Y. I enjoy meeting people there, but every time someone gets friendly with me, I withdraw. I know they wouldn't like me if they got to know me, so I freeze up. I wish I could change."

If Roger really wanted to do something about his problem, he'd have to do more than "wish" for a change. He would have to make the active effort. The first old pattern he has to look at is his feeling about himself. Where did that come from? Somewhere back in his childhood? He would have to put that childish image behind him and view himself as the adult person he is.

Similarly, an insurance underwriter offers: "Talk about patterns. I'm so stuck in my old ways of doing things, I don't think I could change, if my life depended on it." He paused for a moment and reflected. "Me, I take the same bus at the same time on the same street and go to the same job for over twenty years now. Oh, yeah, and I play golf every Sunday with the same foursome."

Although this insurance underwriter views his life as being in a rut, there's nothing really harmful about the patterns he has set.

After all, your patterns may not be as deeply ingrained as they are in any of these people, but chances are you have some patterns that you would like to take a look at and air out.

Meanwhile, here is a game that had amazing results in one college in New York City. It's called The Brand-New Me Day. Select ahead of time a day on which you will play this game. On the day you have chosen, you must try ten new things that you have never done before, or do something in a way different from the way you have in the past.

In the experiment with the college class, some of the experiences were as simple as walking down a new street to as daring as taking a sky dive. Think about what you might do if you had an assignment to do ten new things you had never tried before.

Here are some of the new experiences those college students listed as part of their Brand-New Me Day.

1. I went roller skating.
2. I went to the zoo.
3. I didn't talk to anybody for two hours.
4. I looked, I mean really looked, at the sky.

90

5. I went to visit my aunt in the hospital.
6. I said, "Hello," to a stranger.
7. I took a bus instead of the subway.
8. I walked my boyfriend home.
9. I went bowling.
10. I went to a museum.
11. I ate sushi (raw fish).
12. I went to a singles bar.
13. I went to Lincoln Center.
14. I played with my little nieces.
15. I went to an X-rated movie.
16. I played Ping-Pong.
17. I told my sister I loved her.
18. I shot a bow and arrow.
19. I taught my little brother how to play chess.
20. I got up at 5:00 A.M.

Try the Brand-New Me Day game for yourself. You don't have to limit your new experiences to ten. See how many new experiences you can have for yourself in one day.

HOW TO SHARE

Remember what Ralph Waldo Emerson said: "The only way to have a friend is to be one."

Spend your energies on being the person/friend you want to be. Don't worry about something you're not. The source of friendship is in yourself. As was said before, "Mature, whole people make the best friends."

After all, you are the one who decides how much of yourself to share. Frequently, people find it easier to share more quickly on a superficial or temporary basis.

One opinion pollster says: "It's amazing what people will tell you. They are willing to confide all sorts of things. The trick is to listen. Give no indication of acceptance or rejection, no judgment whatsoever. People will open up and answer the most intimate questions, because they know the questions are for a purpose. It's like you skip through the first couple of layers of protection that people usually use."

People who find themselves in a common emergency share those moments fully. On November 9, 1965, New York City was plunged into a total blackout. There was a power failure in the northeastern

United States and southeastern Canada. People remember that night with mixed emotions.

One woman says: "I can't remember ever before or after that night when New Yorkers were so friendly, so outgoing, so caring. We all helped each other. We shared our candles, our food, our transistor radios. It was beautiful. That was a true time of sharing in our city." This woman who lived in New York City all her life smiled in happy reminiscence.

"Why, my husband even went out and helped direct traffic with a flashlight. There were so many heroic acts that night, neighbors helping neighbors, yes, but even more unbelievable was how perfect strangers came to each other's aid in stranded elevators, stalled subways. You couldn't believe how some people were stopped cold in a bad place. There were so many heroes that night; even our 'bad-news newspaper' had to admit that the people in this city were pretty terrific during the blackout."

That blackout was an example of sharing that works well. An emergency situation brings out the best in most of us for a short time. Momentary or temporary sharing is easier than a long-term commitment.

Mass gatherings of all sorts promote a communal spirit. The camaraderie of a shared cause temporarily lowers our barriers. For a limited time, we can be part of a greater effort, one member, or part of a whole committed group, for example, the 1982 nuclear protest in New York City, the peace marches, the Save the Whales or Save the Seals groups. In these groups you share yourself in the belief of these ideas or causes. You share with a collective group rather than with an individual.

Many people find it easier to strike up a conversation with someone on a plane than with the co-worker they see every day at the next desk. Temporary relationships offer an immediate sharing, with no responsibility for future exchange.

For example, a salesman from Philadelphia says: "What I like about striking up a conversation is the challenge of connecting with all different kinds of people. I like to talk to the janitor, and find something we have in common. I like to find a level that's comfortable for both of us."

Another salesperson from New Jersey adds these thoughts: "I especially like to talk to a man about his business or his job. I talk to the butcher, the produce man, the electrician, the plumber, the guy who works at the gas station. I can spend an hour in the cheese shop talking about the different kinds of cheese and where they come from. All these people know their own jobs. I talk about their livelihood, and I'm really interested in learning about it. Work interests me. That's the kind of conversation-sharing I do. And, that's the kind of sharing I like."

"I like good conversation, someone who knows what's going on in the world and has worthwhile opinions," says a middle-aged corporate executive. "I like a man I can respect, without involvement. What appeals to me is an intellectual relationship."

Indeed, this executive knows what he likes in a relationship. He offers no false images. He will share himself on one level but not on another. He is not interested in the next level of sharing, self-disclosure.

Self-disclosure should take place only in an environment of trust and acceptance. Furthermore, it is a wise man who holds back with his self-disclosure. True intimacy is possible only when two persons are both willing to share themselves through self-disclosure. This involves a responsibility on both parts. When people know who they are and *are* who they think they are, they can offer their friendship to each other.

People may be able to share whole worlds together, but first they must know their own. For example, how far ought personal feelings go in a friendship? How much self-disclosure is healthy and when can it go wrong?

Before self-disclosure can take place, certain ground rules must be set up. Even though these conditions are rarely discussed between people, you may ask yourself if the ground rules are safely in place before you enter a relationship of self-disclosure.

Ask yourself these questions to discover if the conditions are promising for self-disclosure in the relationship.

CONDITIONS FOR SELF-DISCLOSURE

1. Are you comfortable with the other person and is he with you?
2. Do you agree that you'll put up with each other's shortcomings?
3. Can you agree to disagree and still respect the other's opinion?
4. Do you recognize the common concerns between you?
5. Do you agree to respect each other's trust?
6. Do you realize you have a responsibility to each other?
7. Do you agree that all confidences will be kept?

8. Do you agree that you will be tolerant and nonjudgmental about those confidences?
9. Do you agree to offer guidance to each other without trying to change the other person?
10. If things go wrong, can you forgive and forget?

"Sharing of any kind can be difficult for some people," explains a therapist in a mental hospital. "We all have difficulties with certain people at certain times. But that's a part of life." She paused for a moment and then continued: "Someone who never has any problems bores me. That life runs too smooth."

She went on to describe some of the patients she sees daily in her work. "Isolation is the basis of a lot of mental illness. Most of these people have inadequate skills for making friends. They have developed no support network for themselves. When they feel rejected by one person, they feel rejected by the whole world, and they withdraw. And if they withdraw too far, it's all over."

DEVELOPING RESOURCES

You can develop your own inner resources. You can like the person you are. Develop your own resources to enlarge your choices and possibilities for friends. Devote your energies to being the person you want to be. Take the initiative when you can and be receptive to others. Start to work on breaking down any old patterns that are holding you in a fixed method of meeting the world.

In conclusion, choose your friends wisely and try to be comfortable with yourself.

You are the center of all your friendships—the center of your universe.

CHAPTER 8

Great Beginnings

Have you ever wished you could start a conversation with anyone, anytime, anyplace? Impossible? It's easier than you think. In fact, it's as easy as 1, 2, 3. All it takes is a little know-how and some practice.

Each of us has a favorite topic of conversation—ME. Some people find it the easiest subject in the world. Once that area of conversation is launched, some people can talk indefinitely unless channeled in another direction.

George Bernard Shaw said, "A man's interest in the world is only the overflow of his interest in himself."

The other favorite topic in a two-way conversation is YOU. YOU-ME is what two persons have in common at the given moment in time. Another factor they share at that precise moment is their environment. YOU-ME-HERE. The environment, however, is the topic most easily and most often used for a conversation opener.

"Nice day, isn't it?"

The well-known remark attributed to Mark Twain tells us: "Everybody talks about the weather, but nobody does anything about it."

The weather's probably the safest topic for conversation anyone can think of. Usually it's dull, except when you're expecting a hurricane or a blizzard; unless, of course, you happen to live over the San Andreas fault and you feel a tremor. The reason so many people talk about the weather is it's the one thing everyone has in common. It's the basis of most small talk. It is one topic about which everyone can converse. It is a common denominator with the bus driver, the grocery clerk, or the cop on the beat.

The weather has been a topic for conversation since the spoken word began. It has played a tremendous part in our day-to-day lives. For the farmer, it can still make the difference between a bumper crop and the loss of his livelihood. In turn, the weather influences the price we pay for our groceries in the market.

Some people say the weather affects their personalities. So even though it may seem an unimportant topic, in reality it is something that affects us all. As a topic of conversation, the weather is one thing we all have in common. Each time you begin a conversation, you have these three things in common:

1. Yourself
2. The other person
3. Your environment

The quickest and easiest way to start the conversation is with a question about your general environment. You can even omit the weather this time if you like.

1. When will the tide go out?
2. Have you always lived in the castle?
3. Do you know what those bugs are?

After the general environment, you can move to the more specific with your questions.

1. Do you belong to this club?
2. Are all the subways in New York this noisy?
3. Is this your office building?

Although these opening lines offer a common denominator as well as being safe openers, they're not very exciting, nor would they be considered scintillating conversation.

This kind of talk falls into the category of small talk. It is a necessary beginning and/or can serve as a filler until you get around to risking something more meaningful or important.

On the other hand, there are times when you want to start a conversation with some sparkle and wit.

GENERATING RESPONSES

"My all-time favorite conversation opener is the polltaker gambit," says Brad, an advertising copywriter. "I usually try it with pad and pencil in hand, of course, on an attractive woman. My line goes something like this: 'Excuse me, but I'm taking a poll on what makes men attractive to women. Could you describe your ideal man?' I prompt her with short questions that help the answers. 'Do you like blue eyes? Light-brown hair? Over six feet tall?' "

Brad chuckled at his own ingenuity and continued: "Sometimes I can maneuver the answers so that by the time the interview is finished she has described me to a T. And if she hasn't caught on yet, I introduce myself and add, 'Obviously, I'm your ideal man.' "

Brad likes to get a response from people even if it's not always positive. He likes to generate a retort. He keeps a list of stock questions, which he swears always get an answer. Here are some of the questions he calls "Guaranteed Conversation Starters."

1. What do you think of coed locker rooms?
2. Should marijuana be legalized?
3. Should women be drafted?
4. Would you like to see a woman pope?
5. Would you be willing to donate to the sperm bank?
6. If you could be any famous person, whom would you choose?
7. If you were marooned on a desert island with only one person, who would it be?
8. What's the most outstanding memory of your childhood?
9. What's the favorite story your mother/father told you?
10. Tell me about yourself.

(Add a well-placed sprinkling of the word Why? with any of these questions whenever necessary.)

Brad admits that his favorite question is the last one. When it works, it's the most interesting. Be careful with it, however. It takes careful and gentle prodding and real listening on the instigator's part. Resist the temptation to offer your own similarities or differences.

Certain specific environments or populations can promote conversation as well as hinder it. Environments such as hospitals, libraries, and sometimes museums promote self-imposed limits on conversation.

However, most of us find ourselves in places where conversation is called for. Frequently there is no feedback from the other person or no reason to continue. Nevertheless, we are stuck with someone and must find something to talk about. The reason may be a social obligation, or a favor to someone else, or a family duty. When that happens, you can ease the situation if you give yourself some kind of unique challenge in the conversation.

Here are some of those challenges to help keep the conversation moving.

1. Find out as much as you can about the other person in three minutes. (Time yourself.)
2. Decide the one you're talking to is the most fascinating person you've ever met. Which three of his qualities are the most fascinating?
3. Imagine the person you're talking to is a celebrity you are interviewing for the newspaper. Get the facts.
4. Imagine he is a character from your novel. What are his interests, likes, dislikes? Which will you use?
5. Imagine he is a candidate for President. Find out his views on as many issues as possible. (Decide whether you will vote for him.)

Some people enjoy talking to others wherever they are. For example: "My best friend talks to everybody, no matter where she is. If she is standing in a line, she talks to the people in front and behind her. She's a very voluble extrovert in a nice kind of way," boasts Shirley from Pittsburgh. "My friend has a marvelous outlook on life and people. She thinks that everybody is wonderful. She makes connections easily. She talks to the doorman, the mailman, all the service people, and she knows their problems, their family history. People tell her things all the time. I never knew anybody who had less trouble starting a conversation than she does."

Shirley's friend admits what she does is simple but not easy for everybody. She puts it this way: "I have a real interest in human beings. I try to guess where they're coming from, what motivates them to respond to certain situations. I try to understand them."

Her advice sounds very much like Spinoza's in the seventeenth century. He said, "I have made a ceaseless effort not to ridicule, not to bewail, nor to scorn human actions, but to understand them."

LISTENING

Learn to listen actively with the whole of your being. How many times have you asked a friend, "What did you say?" Active listening is a skill that too few of us have and even fewer practice; although everyone can learn, it takes effort. We listen or hear on two levels: content, or the text, and tone, or the subtext.

Not listening has been the subject for comment in literature and drama through the ages.

98

"It is the disease of not listening, the malady of not marking, that I am troubled withal." (Shakespeare, *King Henry IV, Part 2.*)

Consequently, one sure way to encourage friendship is to show the other person you care by listening carefully. That says you are interested in what the person has to say. Not only must you listen to what a friend says, you must assimilate it and reflect upon it.

When you really listen, you concentrate on the person's thoughts as well as words. Most of us are so busy thinking about what we're going to say next that we miss half of what the other person says. And unless we listen for the subtext as well as the text, we miss even more.

"When it's important to me to catch every word, I have a game I play," says Sheila, a traveler's aid counselor. "It may sound silly, but I tell myself the person speaking is a Russian spy and I will have to repeat this conversation to someone in the FBI. I listen very carefully."

Another trick to promote active listening is the one a salesman named Charlie practices. "I paraphrase," he says. "I paraphrase what the other person says as he goes along. For example, if a customer says: 'Try me again next season, Charlie, I might be able to buy the wools then. Who knows? Things may get better; they can't get worse. Right?' I'll say something like, 'I won't forget to check these wools out with you next season.'

"That way I have to listen carefully and I'm sure I understand what the other person means." He paused and then said proudly, "Even when I'm not trying to sell something, my friends all say I'm a good listener."

Therefore, one trick to listening closely is hearing what actors call the *subtext*—the emotion or tone that lies beneath the surface level.

Active listening is a learned skill. When you listen carefully, you really hear other people's opinions about things. You hear facts and opinions that may not agree with your own. But when you listen carefully, you may hear other thoughts and ideas that bear examination. You may discover that some of your opinions cannot stand up to examination. In a sense, it takes courage on your part really to listen to others. You must practice listening often and even put it to the test when the occasion calls for it. It takes courage to risk having your attitudes and opinions changed.

Likewise, sometimes you must see through the dogma of people's words.

"The passion for truth is silenced by answers which have the weight of undisputed authority," Paul Tillich said.

Conversation between friends should be more than just good talk. It should offer a communion of the spirit, a give-and-take of the soul. Listen to the inflection of the words. Try to hear the subtext of the conversation—what lies beneath. A friend knows how to make you feel important, values your conversation and opinions, and if he asks for an opinion, he listens to your advice.

"But when my friend seeks my opinion and I give it, when she doesn't use it, a small piece of me is disappointed," a thirty-five-year-old teacher explains. "I find I am a little more protective of my feelings next time when asked my opinion."

Sometimes people need reinforcement of their own judgment. What they're really asking is, "Don't you agree with my solution to this problem?" In other words, sometimes what they're really saying is, "Tell me what I want to hear."

However, a friend respects the other's opinion. Sometimes the advice is taken, sometimes not. Frequently it is used as part of the evidence. There are people who take an opinion poll among their friends to make up their minds. But whether the opinion or advice is taken, it must be respected and valued for the giving.

G. K. Chesterton said: "There is a great man who makes every man feel small. But the real great man is the man who makes every man feel great."

GETAWAY LINES

Youngsters use the perfect getaway line. When they want to leave a place or a person, they suddenly hear that all-knowing voice. "I have to go home, my mother's calling me." That does it every time. No one else has to hear the call, it's understood the child will leave now.

There are times when we as adults must be more inventive in order to make a graceful exit. We have all been stuck someplace in a conversation with someone we'd rather not stay and talk to. How to leave without offending the person we're with or without offending the host or hostess, that's the question.

For example, one quick getaway that demands fast action and no hesitation is a fast glance at your watch, an audible gasp, and a hurried explanation on your way out. The key words are " ... so sorry ... didn't notice the time ... appointment ... forgive me

. . . late . . . see you again—" all said as you move to the door and out.

If you want to be more graceful but less speedy with your exit, here are some lines that are easier to deliver but will still do the trick:

1. "I must leave before I learn all your secrets. You're absolutely fascinating. Just too much to take in in one evening." (One or all three, depending on how fast you want to leave.)
2. "It's much too late to try to absorb any more of your charming conversation."
3. "My friend's leaving, and I promised to share a cab."
4. "Excuse me, it's time for my medication."
5. " 'Parting is such sweet sorrow, That I shall say good-night till it be morrow.' " (You may give Shakespeare credit or not—it's your choice.)

No one likes to offend another person or be offended, especially not on purpose. So, if the other person is a bore, a white lie is acceptable (by both parties) to maintain the dignity of the situation.

Remember what Spinoza said about his "effort not to ridicule, not to bewail, nor to scorn human actions, but to understand them."

On the other hand, how about the right words for those times when you really hate to leave; those times when you do enjoy the conversation and/or the beginning of a friendship? How do you tell the other person you'd like to know him better?

"Why not say it—'I'd like to know you better'?" says a computer programmer in New Jersey. "It's the most direct sentence I know. It says exactly what I mean, and no beating around the bush."

When you'd like to continue a relationship, but must leave—for whatever reason—tell the person. Pick out something you particularly like about that person and tell him or her so. For example:

"I like the way you think."
"I really enjoy your sense of humor."
"Nobody else makes me laugh the way you do."
"You're so easy to talk to. I enjoyed it."
"I enjoyed your company."
"This was fun. I'd like to see you again."

Simple enough? Each of these lines will tell the other person that you enjoyed the association. You have not asked for any comment or commitment. Therefore, no acceptance or rejection is called for.

You simply expressed your honest enjoyment of that moment in time with that person. That is a good beginning for any friendship.

NEW PLACES—NEW PEOPLE

Sooner or later most people are in the position of being the newcomer. You go to a different location and meet all new people. Finding compatible associates in that situation can be difficult. There are those rare folk, like the woman from Pittsburgh described earlier in this chapter, who have a natural outpouring of human kindness. That natural outpouring works for them wherever they go, but that quality is the exception rather than the rule.

In pioneer days, and even more recently, when a new family moved in, the neighbors called and greeted the newcomers, made them feel welcome. Not so today in most parts of the country. With our highly mobilized society, we see moving vans on the streets and highways every day. People change residences, jobs, and mates as often as Grandma changed the linens. With each of these alterations in one's life comes a new set of friends and/or acquaintances.

"It's no fun to be the new kid on the block," says Marge, a thirty-year-old statistician. "You must wait for the old guard to accept you, or at least for one of them to make the overture."

She stopped for a moment and weighed her words carefully. "I'm recently divorced. I took this job to live in a new city. There's nobody here I know from my old life, so I'm on my own. I have to be careful, because—believe it or not—a lot of these people hold that old stereotype of the divorcée."

How does Marge handle her status? She goes on to say: "I do something new every Sunday—go to a museum, the zoo, a historical landmark, even the ball game. Sunday is my day to experience something new. I've joined a church; my college has an alumni group; and I bowl once a week on the office team. What's my status? Busy, that's what. But I make myself available to others and I try to be friendly. What more can I do?"

Marge has the right idea. She is actively trying to meet new people and discover all she can about her new place.

An older woman in South Carolina, who recently retired to that state, retains her pioneer spirit. "I make pies, cakes, all kinds of things. I take something to someone who's shut in or ill just about every day. Sometimes I take cookies to the Sunday school class or to a meeting. That's my way of reaching out. It's a pretty obvious

102

way, I know. It says: 'I have something to give you. Please take it.' I only hope folks see it's more than my pies and cakes I want them to accept. It's me. I offer my pies and cakes because I know I do those well—it's something everybody appreciates. I've already met lots of nice people and not just the ones I've taken food to, but friends of friends, etc."

In fact, one danger in a change of environment is that of equating the environment with the people. If you remember small towns with dull, provincial people, you may respond to the people in another small town the same way. The logic at work here is this:

1. People in small towns are dull and provincial.
2. This is a small town.
3. All these people are dull and provincial.

Consequently, this behavior will create barriers to communication and friendship. The person who thinks like this may not be aware that he is responding to the place and not to the person.

Likewise, we sometimes respond to the words rather than to the person. We also have stereotypes about certain phrases. What images of people do these conversational phrases call to mind?

"Saints preserve us."
"Pleased to meet you."
"Well, I never—"
"He'll talk your ear off."
"My dogs are barkin'."

Frequently, when one of these phrases or one like it comes up in conversation, an instant impression occurs about the person who said it.

However, now is the time for more conversation. In order for the stereotype to be examined and quickly dispatched, if possible, keep up the conversation. Good conversation can bring about new feelings regarding the person.

Indeed, W. Somerset Maugham claimed that "conversation is one of the greatest pleasures in life."

Hughes Mearns, in his book *Creative Power,* writes: "You have something to say. . . . Something of your very own. Try to say it. Don't be ashamed of any real thought or feeling you have. Don't undervalue it. Don't let the fear of what others may think of it prevent you from saying it. Perhaps not aloud, but to youself. You have something to say, something that no one else in the world has ever said in just the way of saying it."

Learning to explore another human being through dialogue is one of the greatest adventures in life. Too often we settle for the mundane, when with a little encouragement others are quite willing to discuss what's important to them, important to their lives. What are some ways to crack through small talk, to explore the many facets of another person?

Walt Whitman said, "I contradict myself, (I am large, I contain multitudes)."

Yes, each of us contains *multitudes*. The trick is to get past the small talk to the great talk.

Conversation is a way to show another person that you care about him, that you care about what he has to say.

Therefore, caring is the first step in preparing for meaningful dialogue. When you care about the other person, you make him feel important. You listen to what he says and try to lead him one step at a time to a more meaningful level of dialogue.

Here are three sample dialogues. Pick out the line in each of them that maneuvers the dialogue to a more meaningful level.

DIALOGUE 1

PAT: Hi, my name is Pat.

AMY LOU: Mine's Amy Lou. I'm from Atlanta.

PAT: Atlanta, eh? I was there once. That's where they have that beautiful performing arts center, isn't it?

AMY LOU: Yes, it's beautiful. We went to a concert there once.

PAT: What kind of music do you like?

AMY LOU: Jazz, mostly, but I guess I like all kinds.

PAT: How does jazz make you feel?

AMY LOU: Make me feel? I don't know. Why?

PAT: Because some music, one song in particular, makes me feel like I can do anything in the world I want to. Does any music make you feel that way?

AMY LOU: I never thought about it.

PAT: What does give you that feeling?

Of course, the line that pivots the conversation is, "How does jazz make you feel?" and with each succeeding line thereafter Pat tried to elicit a meaningful level in the dialogue. So far, Amy Lou is sidestepping any self-disclosure or meaningful dialogue. She may be cautious, doesn't want to converse on this level, prefers small talk, or simply doesn't think any deeper.

In this next dialogue, the effort comes much sooner.

DIALOGUE 2

JIM: Hi, my name is Jim Johnson. Did you know that there are more Johnsons than any other name in the Manhattan phone book?

TOM: No. I didn't know that. My last name is Jedriewski. There are only four of those, and we're all related.

JIM: Then I'll bet you have no trouble knowing *who* you are.

TOM: What do you mean?

JIM: Well, for example, I'll bet you know one thing you're best at, right?

TOM: Yes, I guess.

JIM: Well?

TOM: Well, what?

JIM: What's the one thing you're best at?

TOM: Oh, swimming, I'm a good swimmer. I dive—scuba, when I can.

JIM: What's it like underwater?

TOM: Great. It's another world.

JIM: Tell me about it. What do you see? What do you feel?

TOM: It's hard to explain.

JIM: Try.

In this dialogue, Jim started out immediately by offering some information about himself. It added name reinforcement to both. Jim made Tom feel important with his next line and carefully led him to the point where he may be ready to discuss something meaningful. Tom is friendly, but in the beginning he parries each effort to bring the dialogue to a more meaningful level. Now he may feel safe enough to move a step farther.

Take a look at the next dialogue. The resistance here is much stronger and out in the open.

DIALOGUE 3

SALLY: This is the worst party I've ever been to.

JACK: Oh, do you think so?

SALLY: You bet I do. I've never met a bigger bunch of bores.

JACK: I don't like bores either. Actually, I like people who make me laugh.

SALLY: I don't know any jokes, and the ones I heard tonight I wouldn't repeat.

JACK: Where would you rather be right now if you could be anyplace in the world you wanted to?

SALLY: Acapulco . . . lying on a beach in the sun.

JACK: Hey, that's one thing we have in common. I love Acapulco too. I wonder what else we have in common. What do you like to do?

SALLY: Anything but stand here and talk.

JACK: Then give me your hand.

SALLY: What?

JACK: Let me see your hand. I'll read your palm. Then all you have to do is stand here and listen.

SALLY: All right.

Jack had an uphill battle all the way with this dialogue. Sally was negative from the moment the conversation began. And it's always easier to communicate negative feelings. Had Jack been a different kind of person, less secure in his own positive outlook, Sally's negative feelings might have swung him over to her way of feeling about the party. Jack is moving from one level of communication to another—touch. With touch, perhaps he will make a connection.

Jack tried humor first, which usually is a good bridge from one level to another. But that didn't work. Not everyone can be funny or even tell a joke. But all of us can remember the funniest thing we ever saw, or the funniest thing we ever did. And even if "you had to be there," as they say, the effort to bring these thoughts and memories into the conversation can put people in the mood for humor. We've all had the experience when something tickled our funny bone, and we couldn't stop laughing. What one person finds funny tells a lot about that person. Can you share the same sense of humor with someone you've just met? Do you laugh at the same things?

Here are some practice dialogues to complete. See if you can continue the level of conversation with lines of your own to keep the dialogue on a meaningful level. Read the dialogue aloud, do both parts, or ask a friend to do it with you. Each of you read a part. You continue the dialogue when the script stops.

106

DIALOGUE 1—TO COMPLETE

You: Hello, my name is _____ and you look like someone I'd like to meet.

OTHER: Well, thanks. My name is _____.

You: You look like a Marilyn (or whatever name the other person said).

OTHER: I do, why?

You: Because I always have at least three things in common with every Marilyn I know.

OTHER: Oh, what do we have in common?

You: I don't know. Let's find out. What do you like to do?

OTHER: I like books, reading, and writing mostly.

You:

(Continue the dialogue from here.)

DIALOGUE 2—TO COMPLETE

OTHER: Hello, my name is Maude. Is this your first time here at our meeting?

You: Yes. My name is _____ and I'm from _____.

OTHER: How do you like it here?

You: Fine, so far. The people seem friendly.

OTHER: We try. But with so many new faces, it's hard to meet everyone.

You: I know. But your face is easy to remember because you have the bluest eyes I've ever seen.

OTHER: I do?

You: Yes. I always try to pick out three things I like about someone to help me remember them. With you it's your eyes, your dress, and your smile.

OTHER: Well, thank you.

You: Want to try it with me? It can be any three things you notice about me.

OTHER: Oh, I don't know if I—

You:

(Continue the dialogue from here.)

DIALOGUE 3—TO COMPLETE

You: I have a problem.

OTHER: Don't we all.

You: But you can solve mine.
Other: Yes, how?
You: I don't know anyone in this whole place. My name is
_____. What's yours?
Other: It's Harold.
You: I'll bet you don't solve many people's problems as easily
as that.
Other: No, I don't.
You: What do you do best, Harold?
Other: Me? Nothing. I'm not good at anything.
You: Well, what one thing do you wish you did better?
Other: I wish I could talk to people better.
You: You're doing fine.
Other: You're asking all the questions.
You: Then why don't you ask me one?
Other: What?
You: Anything. What do I do best or wish I did better?
Other: O.K., what do you do best?
You:
(Continue the dialogue from here.)

Try these three practice dialogues several times to see in how many different directions they can go. See how long it takes you to reach a meaningful level.

Start your own collection of opening lines. Practice them every chance you get. You'll soon learn which ones work for you and which ones don't.

Remember to encourage the other person to talk. Good dialogue is a give-and-take between two persons. Don't offer an answer that ends the conversation. Keep it moving. Encourage the other person to share his opinions, thoughts, ideas, dreams. And listen, really listen to what he says.

Every human being is a gold mine, full of the treasures of good talk. Therefore, take the time and have the patience to dig deep and carefully. You will be rewarded with conversation that brings an understanding of humanity that is one of life's greatest riches.

CHAPTER 9

How to Be a Friend

The best advice on how to be a friend is as simple as this: Be the friend you'd like to have.

Friendship is a two-way street. You can't *have* a friend unless you *are* a friend. To be a friend to another you must first be a friend to yourself. As Honoré de Balzac said, "Nothing is a greater impediment to being on good terms with others than being ill at ease with yourself."

So then, the first prerequisite for being a friend is to accept yourself as you are. Shakespeare wrote,

> Who is it that says most? Which can say more
> Than this rich praise, that you alone are you?
> (Sonnet 84)

Consequently, people who like themselves usually have no trouble in finding others to like.

A friend named Michael offers this thought: "Friendship is the great paradox. It is the need to reaffirm one's existence by the very act of giving oneself to someone else."

Each of us gives different facets of ourselves to others. We all have a combination of personality traits; some admirable, some not so admirable. That is a part of being human. That humanity is what sets us apart from all other creatures and allows us our special relationships with one another.

Samuel Johnson reminded us of this unique quality with his "Friendship: An Ode."

> Friendship, peculiar boon of Heav'n,
> The noble mind's delight and pride,

To men and angels only giv'n,
    To all the lower world denied.

You are special, not perfect perhaps, but unique. You are the only YOU in the entire universe. You can make your friendship something very special and keep it a special part of your life.

Friendship is not a state of being. You don't arrive there and forget about it. It's a constantly changing, shifting, growing process. It must be continually cared for and nurtured. Remember that friendship calls for caring and sharing on both sides. It calls for acceptance of yourself as a person as well as the acceptance of your friend as he or she is. You don't have to "put your best foot forward" all the time.

In other words, don't pretend you're someone more interesting, more important, or more anything. If you will be a friend, let it be the real you. Let your genuine spontaneity come through. Allow your sensitivity and understanding to show. Be yourself.

Consequently, then, the first step in how to be a friend is *acceptance*. Accept yourself as you are.

Be yourself doesn't mean you must be one-sided or one-dimensional. We all have many facets to our personalities. So the advice, "Be yourself," can sometimes be more difficult than it sounds.

E. E. Cummings explains the difficulty this way: "To be nobody—but yourself—in a world that is doing its best, night and day, to make you like everybody else—means to fight the hardest battle which any human being can fight, and never stop fighting."

A playwright named Marlene explains: "That's what I like about having several friends. They all see something different in me. Actually, they each like a different part of my personality. One friend loves to go to the theatre with me, so we can talk all about the play afterward. Another friend is the one who likes my homemaker self. She considers me the domestic expert, or at least the last word, on gourmet recipes. The third is my collaborator. We share our life of the mind. She'd probably be bored to death with either one of the other facets of my personality."

WAYS TO STRENGTHEN YOUR FRIENDSHIP

Being a friend takes more effort than having a friend. Both roles require active participation, however. In order to be a friend, you must continually seek ways to strengthen that friendship. That is a part of nurturing.

110

Step 1. *Accept yourself.* A good initial step in the active nurturing of a relationship is acceptance.

Step 2. *Accept your friend as he or she is.* Accept the differences as well as the similarities. Just as you have many elements about yourself that you had to accept, you must accept your friend in the same way.

Remember how important the quality of loyalty is in all friendships. "Someone I can trust" is the phrase repeated most often.

Step 3. *Be trustworthy.* Be that trustworthy someone for your friend. Be the one he can always trust. There are many ways you can offer that trust to a friend. One of the ways you can help build trust is to be supportive. What are the supportive assets people bring to strengthen their friendships?

"I stand up for my friend," says David from Philadelphia. "I won't listen to any negative criticism about him from anybody. I simply say, 'I don't want to hear it,' and I don't listen. It doesn't matter whether it's true or not. I don't allow other people to put him down or put obstacles in the way of our friendship." David understands the importance of loyalty and acts accordingly.

Step 4. *Be supportive.* "I encourage mutual respect," offers Laura, a thirty-five-year-old editor. "I demonstrate regard for the other person's well-being. 'How are you? What's going on in your life? What are your cares, your concerns?' I'm really interested. I guess you could say I'm a devoted friend. I bring honesty, caring, and patience as my supportive assets."

Step 5. *Show you care.* A stage designer offers this advice on how to show a friend you care: "Show your friend that you care about him just being alive, being on this earth. Show him his life is as important to you as it is to him. You cannot feel alone as long as you have that feeling. You will always be there for him emotionally. Let him know he is not alone in this world."

Step 6. *Share experiences.* "Do things that help your friend feel good about himself," suggests a young doctor named Ben. "Lift him up. I like to compliment people, to make them feel good. I look for the good things. I talk about them. It's not just a compliment, but an appreciation of sincere effort. A friend of mine gave a speech to the medical society, and he did a terrific job. I told him so. I said: 'That was a great speech, especially the way you included all that statistical data and still made it interesting. You had them rolling in the aisles while they were learning new information. What a technique.'"

Notice how the doctor phrased his compliment. It was genuine, with specific areas of excellence singled out.

Let your friend know you appreciate his achievement or thoughtfulness. Share the experience with him. Take an active part in his successes.

No one's life runs smoothly all the time. When things go wrong, don't dwell on it. Learn to overlook the traits in your friend that bother you or annoy you. Remember the second step—accept him.

One of the best ways to strengthen a friendship is to open new areas of the world for that person, to show him new opportunities for discovery or success. Expand his world. People who bring out the best in each other grow in ways that benefit both.

We all remember that certain person who first taught us how to do something, no matter what it was. Who can forget the one who taught you how to ride a bike, dance, or even eat artichokes?

"A friend is a person who shares his knowledge with you. She expands your world in some way. She makes a conscious effort to help you grow. That's how to strengthen a friendship—share what you know," adds a woman from Pennsylvania.

Step 7. *Be a good listener.* "Know what I bring to a friendship? An ear. I've got a long-suffering ear. I will listen to someone talk forever. A guess you'd say what I bring is being a good listener," says Bill from Colorado.

Step 8. *Be sensitive to your friend's needs.* "Don't come on like gangbusters when you know your friend is down in the dumps. He wants you to sympathize with him; read his wavelength. If you are insensitive to his feelings, you don't really care about him or you're too wrapped up in yourself," explains Margo, a psychologist in New York.

Step 9. *Be objective.* This step is a little more difficult. To be objective you must combine the ability of acceptance along with the objectivity. Help your friend see alternate solutions to a problem. When she is emotionally involved with such a dilemma, oftentimes she cannot see her options clearly. One of the ways you can be a friend is be objective, to help her work through the problem. This kind of objectivity usually goes hand in hand with responsibility.

Step 10. *Live joyfully or joyously.* The French have a word for it—*joie de vivre!* Even though Step 10 may be icing on the cake, it's a great way to be a friend.

112

"I try to bring my joy of life of each and every day, every minute to a friendship. I'm a happy person, and I try to share that joy—that happiness—with my friend," declares Patty from Pennsylvania.

To summarize, the ten steps to be a friend are:

1. Accept yourself.
2. Accept your friend.
3. Be trustworthy.
4. Be supportive.
5. Show you care.
6. Share experiences.
7. Be a good listener.
8. Be sensitive.
9. Be objective.
10. Live joyously.

Although the ten steps above represent the ideal, they are hardly a complete list. We all bring different strengths to our relationships. What are some of the positive qualities that you bring to a friendship? Remember, no one brings them all!

YOUR FRIENDSHIP STRENGTHS

What strengths do you bring to a friendship? Put a check mark in the columns below. Give yourself 5 points for USUALLY, 3 points for SOMETIMES, and 1 point for SELDOM.

	USUALLY	SOME- TIMES	SELDOM
Loyalty			
Cheerfulness			
Honesty			
Dependability			
Sympathy			
Intelligence			
Happiness			
Sense of humor			
Fun-loving			

Discretion	————	————	————
Understanding	————	————	————
Compassion	————	————	————
Sensitivity	————	————	————
Sincerity	————	————	————
Good listener	————	————	————
Good conversationalist	————	————	————
Flexibility	————	————	————
Tolerance	————	————	————
Confidence	————	————	————
Wide variety of interests	————	————	————

A total of 80 points or more indicates you know how to be a friend. You bring many strengths to a relationship. A score of 60 to 70 shows you bring the average strengths to the friendship. Anything below 60 means you need more support from others than you give in a friendship.

RESPONSIBILITY IN FRIENDSHIP

"Friendship is always a sweet responsibility, never an opportunity." (Kahlil Gibran.)

Chapter 4 explored what your expectations were in a friend, but what do you expect from yourself as a friend? What are the standards you set for yourself? Are they realistic?

"I demand tolerance from myself," says a realtor in Ohio. "I expect it in others, so it is very important that I reciprocate. I try to get rid of pettiness and selfishness in myself, especially when it comes to being a friend."

Some of us set standards for ourselves in a friendship that we'd never expect from anyone else. We demand from ourselves a loyalty, tolerance, and acceptance that very few human beings are capable of. Loyalty is the all-important quality in a friendship, but blind loyalty can be stupidity if that loyalty is misplaced.

114

"I expect nothing from myself or anyone else. When a relationship occurs, I'm pleasantly surprised." This speaker, a computer operator named Paul, paused and then added, "With no risk, there's no pain!"

What are the responsibilities in a friendship? What responsibility do you give to your friends? When asked for an opinion, do you always give it? Sometimes, when a friend asks for an opinion, he really doesn't want it; be noncommittal. Give the problem—the responsibility—back to him. There are times when you must weigh and balance which of you has the responsibility for the decision. It makes more sense to help the person see both sides of the problem, so he is better equipped to make his own decision. It's better to help a friend make his decision than to make it for him.

Understand the difference between responsibility and blaming. You are responsible for your own actions. It is important to understand the responsibility involved in any relationship. People who are the most responsible are willing to take more risks in a friendship, take it to the deeper level. You must be able to distinguish the behavior of the person from the person himself. When your friend disapproves of something you do, separate the action from the person. But take responsibility for your action by saying, "I was wrong in that action, and I will deal with that behavior."

Oftentimes the way that approval or disapproval is stated is all that's necessary to separate the action from the person. For example, rather than "You're stupid to do that" one can say, "That was a stupid thing to do."

You may not approve of your friend's actions, but you do approve of her. Make that clear in your communication.

"You drink too much!" (A judgment of the person.)
"You drank too much at the party last night." (A judgment of a particular action at a specific point in time.)
"You're rude and a loudmouth!" (A judgment of the person.)
"I'm sure you shouted louder than you realized when Mrs. Jones was here. She probably thought you were rude." (This sentence puts the focus back on the behavior rather than on the person.)

You might prefer to approach the incident from the positive angle: "You're usually so polite to Mrs. Jones. It's a shame you had to lose your temper and shout at her today."

Or: "I wish you'd try to control that anger. Anger makes me very nervous," rather than: "Stop that raving. You make me nervous."

Whenever possible, look for your friend's assets. Most people are quick to notice faults. Take some time and ask yourself, "What are her good qualities?"

Another responsibility in friendship is for both parties to forgive and forget. Give up your grievances. Everyone hurts and is hurt by a friend at some point in life. Very few of us deliberately set out to hurt a friend, but it happens, even when we don't mean it to. No two persons can exist in total harmony all the time.

Consequently, there are times in a friendship when you reach an impasse. At those times you must agree to disagree, and if necessary, bring in a third party to act as mediator.

Furthermore, learn to give up your grievances. Forget the hurt. What hurts? Neglect hurts. Abandonment hurts. Refusal hurts. The sooner you can forgive and forget, the quicker the relationship can continue where it left off.

Don't exchange your grievance for the feeling of self-sacrifice. Too much sacrifice in a friendship can have a negative effect. Don't sacrifice so much for a friend that you make him feel guilty. A friend feels guilty, not grateful, because what he gets comes not from love but self-denial. No one really wants the fruits of someone else's self-denial.

Here are ten sentences every friend should keep in his or her vocabulary and *use* regularly:

1. I'm sorry.
2. I didn't mean it that way.
3. I understand.
4. Forgive me?
5. I forgive you.
6. You're a good friend.
7. How can I help?
8. I know how you feel.
9. What do you think?
10. I'm with you.

To be a friend, here are ten lines to *eliminate*:

1. I told you so.
2. It was all your fault.
3. How could you be so stupid?
4. How could you do such a thing?

5. I don't care *what* you say.
6. Who needs you?
7. You're the one to blame.
8. Don't you know anything?
9. You made me do it.
10. You'll never understand.

Most people have their own test for friendship, some way to decide whether they will be a friend to the person or not.

"My test is simple," says a builder from California. "I ask myself, 'Do I trust the person?' Am I willing to risk the possibility of rejection and hurt? If I think the relationship is worth it, I risk. If not, I don't. It's that simple."

A well-known author says: "Test of friendship? I guess it's that I trust that person tee—totally. If I was down-and-out, I know she wouldn't rot on me. That's my test."

"One thing I can't stand," states a college professor from New Jersey, "is a friend who thinks he has to psychoanalyze you. Friends don't psychoanalyze you, they accept you. They accept your nature without asking all kinds of intimate questions. So my test for a friend would be, 'Can I accept the person—as is?' "

LONG-TERM FRIENDSHIPS

Long-term friendships embody some unique and often universal qualities. The ability to maintain a long-term friendship takes special nurturing on both sides of the friendship. At certain times one person does most of the nurturing, at another time the pendulum swings, and the other person takes over. Sometimes one person makes most of the effort. For those who cherish long-term friendships, it doesn't matter. They seem more willing to make the effort all the time.

There is never a question of loyalty in this relationship. That quality has been proved through the test of time. There is no question of reciprocity, it is taken for granted. The old friend understands when you can't see him. And, when you do, it is quality, rich time together.

"Friendship is one of the most important things in my life. It's one of the greatest gifts we have. I especially enjoy long-term friendships," explains Vallery from the Bahamas. "I've never lost a friend. The ability to enjoy being open, as well as the ability to enjoy the openness of the other person, is there. No judgment is involved, only acceptance."

Most long-term relationships have seen the friends through happy times as well as sad. Many times a period of grief has been worked through together. Ways to share both the good times and the bad have been discovered.

Loyalty in a long-term friendship involves maintenance of the relationship. When you make the effort to keep in touch, you show your acceptance of the individual. Your maintenance shows. When she goes out of her way to let you know you're in her thoughts, she shows maintenance to the relationship also.

"I think we care more about a relationship in which we learned something—something important in our lives," points out a biologist from California. "You remember the friend who shared a vision of the universe with you. Someone who opened your eyes to a whole new way of thinking and seeing."

Many aspects of ourselves we discover through our friend's eyes. "I have a friend I've known for twenty-five years," the biologist continues. "She had more faith in my abilities when we were growing up than I did. She believed in me. She still does. That kind of devotion and faith is something I'll never forget. It doesn't matter one little bit that now I do most of the keeping in touch, since we're three thousand miles apart. I do that gladly to maintain the friendship."

A recurring pattern shows up in a long-term friendship. Just as loyalty is the overwhelming quality everyone seeks in a friend, the quality found in a long-term friendship is acceptance. With that comes a belief in mutual growth.

Therefore, the acceptance takes on a broader meaning. The acceptance is not just of what the person is now—but of what he will become. A commitment to growth is cherished on both sides.

Oftentimes in a long-term friendship, one person will give more of himself than he receives. One friend may have a greater need for emotional support at that point in time than the other. This is understood between friends. You shore me up when I need it, and I do the same for you when you need it.

Another recurring element in the long-term friendship is absence of competition. Real friends don't compete. There is no need for competition between them. You enjoy each other's successes. You can be equally as happy for a friend's success as for your own.

Other qualities shared in long-term relationships are dignity and respect. Each person respects the dignity of the other. There is no need to share all the details of the other person's life. There are acknowledged boundary lines dignified in the relationship.

118

"Some skeletons are better left in the closet," exclaims an old friend from Philadelphia.

What assets do you bring to a long-term friendship?

Sally, an executive secretary, says: "I accept the person as she is, and I will be a friend. I'll be there when she needs me. I'll support her, lift her up, applaud her efforts. I'll be there for her in every way I can. And I'll appreciate her own good qualities. I'll be a believer—that means I'll believe in what she can be."

Warren, an accountant from Detroit, says: "I practice *image-building*. You know, 'Love thy neighbor as thyself.' I really try to do for the other person what I'd like someone to do for me. I'm very supportive. Each friendship is unique in what I bring to it—but I always bring energy."

Janet, a druggist in Maryland, says: "I try to give empathy first, then comes humor, intelligence, and loyalty—unless proven otherwise. I try to tune into the other person's need. When you want someone available to you, and he can't be there, you understand. I try to be there for the other person."

Hal, a doctor in Ohio, says: "I'm ridiculously accessible. I'll be there when needed. I'll go out of my way for a friend. It's hard to find someone who's willing to do the same. But I don't expect what I'm not willing to give back. When a friend moves away, I try to stay in touch. I write to him. I try to keep that person involved in the important things in my life in every way I can."

Marilyn, a teacher from New Jersey, says about long-term friendships: "Any friend of mine has to have a sense of humor, a resiliency, a strength. Friendship is like a marriage. It's compromise. That's a vital ingredient in any long-term relationship: *compromise*. A long-term friendship is nurtured by common interests, and by sharing in the same dreams and aspirations."

Frequently the qualities found in a long-term friendship are the same ones found in any friendship. However, they have passed the test of time, which gives them added validity. These qualities are usually found among the following:

1. Mutual acceptance
2. Mutual growth
3. Lack of competition
4. Respect and dignity
5. Unquestioned loyalty
6. Common interests
7. Mutual support

8. Accessibility (not necessarily physical)
9. Shared dreams and aspirations
10. Ability to compromise

There may be other qualities you value as well. What would you add to this list? Include the ones that have value for you from this list and add your own.

A youngster was overheard at a wishing well. He said, "God, please make me be the kind of person I'd like to have for a friend."

Who could ask for anything more?

CHAPTER 10

Enjoying Your Own Company

We spend time learning about so many things: our universe, our world, its cultures, its people. Why is it we spend so little time in the exploration of our own private universe—the self? The single most important person in your life is YOU. You are the center of your universe.

Take some time out and say "Hello" to yourself. Take an afternoon off, spend an evening alone, go to breakfast with yourself. When was the last time you scheduled "do nothing" time?

Give yourself a treat. Spend some time doing something alone that you really enjoy doing. Get in touch with the YOU in your life. Don't feel guilty. Enjoy the fact that you are taking time out for yourself.

Cervantes put it this way: "Make it thy business to know thyself, which is the most difficult lesson in the world."

How many times have you asked yourself, "Did I do that?" or thought to yourself, "That isn't like me." Few people take the time to find out who they are or what they are like, to discover the self, to appreciate the self.

WHO AM I?

There is a party game called Who Am I? In this game one player decides on a famous person he will be. The other players ask him questions for clues to his identity that can be answered "Yes" or "No." If a direct question is asked, the first player must be able to give an answer without giving away his Who Am I? For example:

PLAYER 2: Are you in politics now?
PLAYER 1: Yes.

121

PLAYER 2: Are you the leader of a major nation?
PLAYER 1: Yes.
PLAYER 2: Are you the leader of the British Empire?
PLAYER 1: No, I am not Margaret Thatcher.
PLAYER 2: Are you the leader in Japan?
PLAYER 1: No, I am not Zenko Suzuki.
PLAYER 2: Are you the President of the United States?
PLAYER 1: Yes, I am Ronald Reagan.

We might ask ourselves the same question. Could you give ten answers to the question "Who am I?"

I am a writer.
I am a director.
I am a commuter.
I am a theatre lover.
I am a weight watcher.
I am an American.

Many people overlook their own best natural resource—themselves. There was a book not long ago entitled *How to Be Your Own Best Friend*. With a whole book devoted to that subject, a great many people must be interested in the how-to part.

Just how can you follow the advice of Cervantes, "Make it thy business to know thyself"? How can you discover what makes you tick? What are some ways to learn about yourself; the who of YOU? Where do you start?

FINDING YOUR SOURCE

Begin by finding your source. What were you like as a child? See if you can find some old pictures, a scrapbook, report cards, whatever is accessible to you from the past. If you don't have a picture, try to bring one into your mind. See yourself as a child. Remember what you were like. Look at the person in the picture objectively. Take a piece of paper and make a list of the good qualities you remember in your child-person. In the opposite column, list some of the nonassets of your person at that particular time.

Let your thoughts flow back in time. What were some goals and dreams of your child-person? Write those down. Again, on the opposite side of the paper, write the concerns, problems, fears you

122

had then. Try to get in touch with the child in yourself. Most of us can find him or her without too much difficulty. Just think about the last time you had a sudden urge to do something, but censored it. You probably told yourself you were being childish. That's the part of you you want to find.

What were some things that child liked to do: games, sports, anything that was fun for him? What did he do well? What was he *pretty good* at? Write those things down too, under LIKES. In the opposite column, write some things your child-person disliked under DISLIKES. What were some things he had to do but hated? (Eat spinach, do homework, wash dishes.) What were some things he did not do well or even passably?

Take a good long look at the paper. Look at your *likes* and *dislikes*. Compare the assets and the nonassets. One thing you can be sure of is you've grown, you've changed; you've matured in many ways, if not in all.

Take another piece of paper. Begin by listing your assets *now*. Ask yourself: "What do I do well? What am I good at?"

Write on the paper, "One thing I do well is _____." See how many things you can think of and add them to your list. Don't stop until you have at least ten things, even if it's something like "wax the floor" or "wash the car."

Think about some things you'd like to do better. Below your DO WELL list, make your DO BETTER list. "One thing I'd like to do better is _____." Allow yourself to list only half as many things on your DO BETTER list as you put on your DO WELL list.

Take a careful look at this list and be grateful for yourself. In the words of William Saroyan, the American playwright: "Be grateful for yourself, yes, for yourself. Be thankful. Understand that what a man is is something he can be grateful for and ought to be grateful for."

LIFE ROLES

Most of us play several roles in our daily lives: mother, wife, friend, etc. Therefore, another facet of "Know thyself" is to know the many roles you play. The more roles you play, the more facets to your "self."

How many roles do you play? Check the ones on this list you play in your daily life. Add any that are not here.

I am a wife. _____

I am a mother. _____

I am a daughter. _____

I am a husband. _____

I am a father. _____

I am a son. _____

I am a friend. _____

I am a teacher. _____

I am a student. _____

I am a neighbor. _____

I am a worker. _____

I am a boss. _____

I am a Democrat. _____

I am a Republican. _____

I am a vegetarian. _____

I am a _____. _____

The roles we play in life change, which gives us an opportunity for a wider variety of experiences.

"I seek out new experiences," says a writer named Patrick. "I love to go someplace completely different from anything I know. I once went down to the Fulton Fish Market in New York at four o'clock in the morning. It was a whole other world: the fishermen with their catch, the buyers, the fish store owners, the restaurateurs. The sights and sounds, the smells—they were all so different from anything I had ever experienced before. Even the language was different. Oh, they spoke English, but there was a different nomenclature. It was fascinating. It was like being in another world in another person's shoes."

Can you put yourself in someone else's shoes and take a look at yourself? Try it. Pick out a friend or acquaintance and take a good look at you, as if you were the friend. If you have a tape recorder available, use it and talk about you as your friend would. If there's no recorder, write a character sketch of you from your friend's point of view. Of course, you can't know exactly how your friend feels about all of your personality traits, but comment on those which you have feedback on and make up the rest.

SUPPORTIVE SELF

Start listening to yourself. Communicate with that self. Allow yourself the pleasure of listening to what you really think; of what you have to say; of what you want to do. How many times when someone asks you what you want to do have you answered, "I don't care"? Of course, there are times when we all go along with someone else's plans or desires, because we care more for the other person than we care about the plans. When that happens, recognize the reason behind your choice. Don't mistake one for the other. That kind of awareness will keep you in touch with yourself, not just bypass your feelings as well as your thoughts.

Give yourself a treat. Listen to what you want to do. The more you can listen to yourself, be in touch with yourself, the quicker you will "know thyself."

People who like themselves find others to like. Do you find yourself an interesting person? There are many ways to help ourselves become more interesting, and have more to offer ourselves and others. What are your special interests and/or hobbies? Interests can work two ways. The interest can come first to learn about a subject, or the subject can trigger your interest.

One woman from Detroit puts it this way: "I wrote an article about a man who was a dog trainer. I didn't know much about dogs when I started. In fact, I really had no interest in dogs. But after I found out how much was involved in their training, I was fascinated. Well, to make a long story short, guess who has a dog now? Right! Not only do I have a dog, but I'm involved in training and showing that dog."

That's an example of the interest coming after the subject. Of course, it's much easier the other way, when the interest comes first. But as you can see, it is not the only way.

For the person who has limited interests and would like to broaden his base of activities and interests, this writer's experience is one to benefit from.

EXPANDING INTERESTS

None of us can be interested in something we know nothing about. We must actively discover some new areas. Most of us can find something we've always wanted to do but never had the time, the money, the opportunity, or whatever our excuse was at that moment. Stop and think of all the things you thought you'd like to do at one time or another.

Here's the list from a forty-five-year-old housewife in Pennsylvania. These are the things she wanted to do then and wants to do now.

1. Go scuba diving
2. Go skydiving
3. Take a CPR course
4. Learn to type
5. Go to museums
6. Learn bridge

She went through her list to see which item or items she could start with. She first took stock of her time, her money, and the opportunity for that activity in her area. She added another consideration, the consideration of her physical self. All these considerations were to be weighed and balanced in her choice of which interest to pursue.

She threw out skydiving first. Although it had been an avid interest when she was younger, she felt that at her present age of forty-five it might be too much for her physically.

Next she discarded scuba diving. At this moment in time the cost of instruction and equipment was prohibitive for her.

Lack of opportunity was the reason she discarded the CPR course. Such a course was offered every summer in her area, but not at this time of the year. That left her with three choices: the typing course, museums, and bridge. She really had no preference as to which she would pursue. So she asked herself which activity might have an additional benefit for her. The answer was bridge. She would learn with other people. She would play the game with others. Bridge offered her the additional advantage of meeting new people.

Make a list of at least six of your interests now or in the past. Put each one to the test: time, money, opportunity, and physical self. Check to see if any of these interests offer an additional benefit.

Travel is one of the most appealing ways to enjoy your own company and experience new places and people. The traveler must be open to a new world. He must grant himself the privilege of looking with a fresh perspective.

Travel doesn't have to mean jet planes and ocean liners, around-the-world cruises, or travel agency trips. Travel can be as simple as going to a local historical point of interest, or the nearest park or lake. Every state has its tourist attractions. People from other parts of the country and the world come there to see those sights. Start your own travels as close as your nearest park. Take a guided tour if offered, along with other tourists.

For those who can afford more expensive travel opportunities, travel is recognized as one of the best ways to broaden your experiences and meet new people. Another way to expand your interests is to *learn* something new. Study a new subject. Take a course in a field you know nothing about. Learn more about a procedure you know slightly. You can even combine travel and study. There's a study tour for everyone's interest from an archaeological dig in Mexico to Haitian art in Haiti. All it takes is time and money.

"I like entertainment; that's my interest," says Marge, a twenty-four-year-old secretary. "But I always go to the same things. I guess to broaden my interests I should try something else. I like music and I go to concerts. Maybe I'll try an opera. I hear that's a whole other world." She laughed and added, "Maybe I should try one of those folk festivals."

Everyone can build on his or her existing interests—try something new. Someone who enjoys a variety of different experiences is someone who attracts others who enjoy any one of those experiences.

You can develop yourself to be a more interesting person, not only for others but for yourself as well. Explore your interests and yourself. You may discover a much more fascinating person inside you than you ever thought possible.

BARRIERS

"So much is a man worth as he esteems himself." (François Rabelais.)

Tons of people are petrified of being alone. When they are alone, they feel abandoned—worthless. Usually this feeling is found in a person who doesn't know he has grown up. He has erected his own barriers to being alone. With his barrier firmly in place, there's no way he can enjoy his own company. If he is never alone any longer than possible, he doesn't have to be aware of himself. During these brief times when he is alone, he acts as though there's someone else there, for example, radio or television on, or he prepares for the time when someone else will be there. He or she will clean the house so that it will be acceptable to another person, bake cookies, or prepare other food. Each of these activities, although practiced alone, is for the express purpose of the offering to another person.

The person who erects barriers to being alone doesn't feel he's really living without another person to share in that living. People who have trouble being alone don't find themselves very interesting. These people usually subscribe to the theory, "Anyone is better than no one."

One young doctor from Pennsylvania puts it this way: "I find I have a need to be entertained. I can't sit in an empty house. Oh, I can go fishing or something like that . . . usually with another person. But I just plain don't enjoy being alone. I end up finding something to do around the house: building something, painting. The things I do are more for the anticipated response from other people than for myself." He paused for a moment as if making a discovery. "What I don't do is think about the growth in myself or appreciate myself as a unique human being."

"I'm rarely satisfied with the self," explains a carpenter from New York. "I avoid thinking about my state of being. I do all these unimportant, 'ditsy' things, rather than what I would choose to do. If I have all these ditsy things to do, I don't have to make any choices."

On the other hand, a flight attendant named Pauline offers this insight into her own needs: "I need private time to refuel the public me. When I'm alone, I can eat sardines and anchovies and not offend anyone."

YOUR OWN COMPANY

Do you enjoy your own company? What do you like to do alone? How do you spend the time alone?

Marlene, a nurse, answers the last question this way: "I love being alone. I relax. I enjoy watching animals, birds—all of nature. I like the trees, the stars, the flowers. It's the best way I know to relax."

An insurance actuary from Texas says: "I love to read alone, or play games like solitaire, or do crossword puzzles. I like to listen to music, write, think, clean, and sometimes do absolutely nothing. I consider time alone a luxury time. Not to have to deal with anybody is ideal."

Jack, who is proud of his eighty-six years, enjoys his time alone. "I like to reminisce, relive some of the past experiences both good and bad. Without the bad, you don't enjoy the good as much."

A public affairs director named Marjorie says: "I once had aspirations to be a ballet dancer. I love to turn on the radio and just dance all over the place."

Nicole from Manhattan adds, "I do things by myself that other people do together, and I have a great time."

Do you enjoy your own company? Try this test. Answer the following questions with USUALLY, SOMETIMES, and NEVER.

1. Do you look forward to an evening alone at home? ____
2. Would you rather stay home with a good book or go out with an acquaintance? ____
3. Do you like to take long walks alone? ____
4. Do you ask a friend to join you in an activity even when you know he doesn't like it? ____
5. Did you ever have a friend you didn't want? ____
6. Do you enjoy eating in a restaurant alone? ____
7. Do you enjoy observing the wonders of nature? ____
8. Do you enjoy silence? ____
9. Do you prefer parties and social gatherings to reading in the library? ____
10. Do you frequently run out of things to do? ____

If your answers to questions 1, 2, 3, 6, 7, 8 were USUALLY and your answers to questions 4, 5, 9, 10 were SOMETIMES or NEVER, you enjoy your own company very much. If, on the other hand, your answers to 1, 2, 3, 6, 7, 8, were NEVER and answers to 4, 5, 9, 10 were USUALLY, you don't enjoy your own company very much.

What are some things people enjoy doing alone? One of the most popular pastimes is to fantasize or daydream. Almost everyone who enjoys being alone enjoys fantasizing and, in turn, enjoys that part of his own company.

A planned fantasy can be a very healthy outlet, as well as a rehearsal for many life situations.

Another popular pastime is to read alone. Other activities listed most often are: listen to music, listen to the radio, watch television, sew, cook, think, organize, plan for the future, evaluate, garden, go to movies, go to restaurants, bicycle, walk, jog.

A politician from New York has a unique pastime when he's alone. "I make lists—lists for everything. I make a list of what I'm going to do in the next twenty minutes or the next twenty years. I make lists of things I want to buy, of courses of study I'd like to take, jobs I want to have. I even make lists of people I'd like to know better. I enjoy putting things down on paper. It gives a validity to what I'm doing."

"I like to arrange things," remarks a television producer named Allan. "I arrange my papers as I arrange my mind. I plan things when I'm alone. I develop concepts. Most of my creative energies function best when I'm alone."

A young woman named Corine says: "My hobby is daydreaming. That's what I like to do when I'm alone. I write many novels in my head. I guess you could say daydreaming is my entertainment. I like being alone a lot."

"I love to be alone. I enjoy my own company," explains a college administrator from Pittsburgh. "I get home at night and close my door and say, 'This is my place and I'm by myself.' It's wonderful. I love it. I dabble around the house and just enjoy being there."

LONELY

Alone is not synonymous with *lonely*. Many people who are alone much of the time are not lonely. The opposite can be true also. People who are constantly surrounded by others can be lonely. According to statistics, more people live alone today than ever before and the number is constantly rising. Some of them thrive on it, while others are miserable.

If the present divorce rate is any indication, many people no longer stay in a dying relationship that offers no joy or satisfaction to either party. They would rather be alone than with someone who makes them miserable.

Every mature human being feels lonely at some time or another in his life. That's human nature. It's when the condition persists that problems arise. A person who can't stand to be alone is someone who has not come to grips with being an adult. The child-adult concept is not mutually exclusive. We can learn from the child within us. There is some of the child in us all. Frequently, the child in you is the one who can give you the most help. There's a small voice that says, "Be good to yourself." The child within says, "It's all right to be lazy, to goof off once in a while." As long as the adult stays firmly in command to remind you of your responsibilities, the things you must do, the child self can contribute to the marvelous combination of you.

"Enjoy the fact that you are taking time out for yourself," offers a young woman from Brooklyn.

130

A widow of some duration offers her thoughts on being alone. "I feel alone (not lonely) most of the time. I'm essentially a happy individual. I love life. I like reading and studying alone, and require some of this each day. I also enjoy many things with or without company, such as walking, art galleries, museums, the theatre."

NO ONE OR ANYONE?

Would you rather have anyone for company than be by yourself? Try this quiz. Find out if you prefer to be alone or be with somebody/anybody. Answer these questions YES, NO, or SOMETIMES:

1. Would you rather go to a concert of music you really don't like with an acquaintance or stay home alone and listen to music you do like? _____
2. Would you rather go to a movie you don't want to see with the girls/guys at the office than stay home and read a book? _____
3. Would you rather go to a singles club or a neighborhood bar than walk by yourself? _____
4. Would you rather go bowling with your next-door neighbor or swimming alone? (Assume you can do both activities equally as well.) _____
5. Would you rather go on a group tour than travel by yourself? _____
6. Would you rather go to dinner with someone you didn't like than eat in a restaurant alone? _____
7. Would you rather ride in a car pool with strangers than drive alone? _____
8. Would you rather spend the evening with someone who complained the whole time than stay home alone? _____
9. Would you rather visit an acquaintance you really didn't like or stay home alone? _____
10. Do you believe somebody/anybody in your life is better than nobody? _____

If you answered YES to 8 or more of the questions, you have great difficulty in being alone. You definitely prefer to be with somebody/anybody. If you answered YES to 6 or more, you prefer being with others, but you can manage alone.

CHOICES

What choices do you have in learning to enjoy your own company? Are there alternatives to the somebody/anybody answer to being alone?

Get in touch with yourself. Ask yourself, "What would I really like to do just for me?" Schedule some time for yourself—time alone. We schedule time with other people. Why not schedule some time for yourself? Give yourself time to do something for yourself. Offer yourself the option of doing something or nothing.

People who have been constantly entertained may not believe they can learn to enjoy their own company, but they can learn.

Begin by looking at the times you are alone. Some blocks of time are easier to handle than others. You probably won't begin to enjoy your own company by staying home on Saturday night, especially if you believe that Saturday night is the time you're supposed to be with somebody.

Select a block of time, a modest block of time for yourself. Do something you enjoy. Concentrate on that activity.

"I don't have to be with someone to enjoy doing the things I like," offers a woman from Pennsylvania. "In fact, sometimes I think we tend to use people to do things with us. It's different if the other person wants to do it with you. But I'd rather not use someone to go along with me, when I can enjoy my plans equally as well alone."

What are some other activities you can practice to help you enjoy your own company?

See yourself as a winner. Visualize yourself receiving whatever it is you dream of. Begin with a good positive fantasy.

Since fantasizing is one of the most popular ways to enjoy being alone, it's a good place to start. Work on it until you can be comfortable with a good positive fantasy.

Here are six good fantasies to try. Picture yourself in each one. Begin with an incident you have already experienced that didn't turn out the way you wanted it to. Imagine the situation exactly the way it was, right up to the point of where you would change it. Now imagine the incident the way you wished it had happened. See the people doing and saying what you want. See yourself in command of the situation. Some people talk out loud to help reinforce their fantasy. Use the technique you are most comfortable with. Act it out

132

for yourself in your imagination or as an improvisation with dialogue.

Try the following fantasies for yourself:

1. The past situation you would change (described above).
2. You take the initiative to make something happen that you desire.
3. Fantasize a situation that is likely to occur at some future time in your life. See yourself handling the situation in a positive way.
4. See yourself as being at the height of fame and success in your line of work.
5. See yourself in the most ideal relationship with someone you admire very much.
6. See yourself being crowned as Miss, Mrs., or Mr. America on the basis of all your talents and good looks.

After you have practiced these fantasies, come up with some of your own. Your imagination is a reward for being human. Learn to value it and use it.

Albert Einstein said, "Imagination is more powerful than knowledge."

"My favorite fantasy is seeing myself as a baseball player, or the manager or coach," admits a thirty-five-year-old lawyer. "That's right up there on my list of favorite fantasies, along with seeing myself as a political candidate, and sometimes even . . . President."

"I fantasize being glamorous and sought after by handsome, rich, famous men," says Sheila, a hairdresser. "I think a lot of women have those fantasies. Sometimes I get ideas for new hairdos from my fantasies. I always see myself wearing a beautiful dress, with a very fancy hair style."

Arthur, a thirty-year-old store manager, offers: "I like to fantasize a fictional friendship. I especially like to fantasize a friendship with someone like Alexander the Great. I'm his right-hand man and help him civilize the East. We talk a lot about Aristotle and his teachings. Oh, it's a grand fantasy."

"I think about famous people too," agrees Howard, a commercial artist. "My fantasy friendship is with Picasso. He was such a ,modernist, but spiritually and emotionally he was a traditionalist. All of his work is shot through his own heart. I sometimes fantasize painting with him and creating something as beautiful and wonderful as he did."

To enjoy your own company, you must get to know yourself. There are many ways to explore you. Perhaps some of the activities mentioned in this chapter are new to you. Try them. Push back your own boundaries. Dare to experiment in the greatest discovery you will ever make. Discover all you can about you.

Then and only then will you learn what Cervantes called "the most difficult lesson in the world": *Know thyself.*

CHAPTER 11

What to Do
When You'd Rather Not Be Friends

"Walk away" is the simplest advice to the question, What do you do when you'd rather not be friends? This advice comes from a sixteen-year-old girl who sees the problem as one with a simple solution. Good advice, direct, and to the point. It certainly is the easiest way to discourage any further association. However, there are times when this action is not possible.

Confucius said, "Have no friends not equal to yourself."

True intimacy is possible only between equals. This equality can take many forms. It is not necessary to be equal professionally, financially, or intellectually, but this equality comes from a deeper base. The equals in friendship accept each other as equal human beings. There must be a mutual understanding and/or agreement of common concerns.

You don't want to be friends with everybody, anymore than everybody wants to be your friend. You want someone you can relate to as an equal. And since we are all unique human beings, we· all have different equals.

Friends who are equal usually have an independent life of their own. Neither one is dependent on the other for that life.

"I like strong, independent people who have a life of their own," says a teacher from Colorado. "I'm pleased to share that life with them, just as I share mine too. But I'm not interested in anyone who is dependent on me."

People who are too quick to reach for others' friendship often-times have a void in their lives to fill. Some people are naturally like that, but others are desperate for someone—anyone. They have no priorities. Most of these people have not yet learned to enjoy their own company. They are looking for the "anyone" who's better than "no one."

Chapter 10 explored the questions: Do you enjoy your own company? and Is anyone better than no one?

There are times in everyone's life when he or she needs someone. A middle-aged writer from Ohio said when she was younger she had trouble doing things by herself. She mentioned some of the ways she used to spend her time, because she thought that's how it should be done. "When I first came to New York I guess I was lonely or didn't know better. Maybe I was just hungry. But anyway—I went out with several different advertising men. One was from Columbus, Ohio. One was from Cleveland, and the rest were from New York. Sure enough . . . I got dressed up, went out to a nice restaurant, and got a free dinner. But I didn't enjoy myself! And I didn't like to have to fight off the guy when we got back to my apartment. I suddenly realized—and it did come suddenly—that I didn't have to accept dates or appointments with people I didn't care about. I could eat at home and enjoy myself much more than getting dressed up (and in those days we counted wearing a tight girdle as part of dressing up), and having an evening out with someone I didn't enjoy being with. I can't believe it, but when that happened, I was already twenty-five!"

Many of us go through the motions with other people, when we would much rather be by ourselves and truly enjoy our own company.

Why do we hesitate to dine out alone? Go to a movie, plays, or anyplace alone? Play games alone? Are we still tied to the old habit of needing a partner to go somewhere? Although women have had this problem much longer and more often than men, it is not really a problem with a sexual connotation. Many men don't enjoy going places alone, but culturally men alone are much more accepted than women.

Once the habit of going with someone is broken, you give yourself a choice: "Do I want to accept this invitation? Would I rather go alone? Would I rather go with someone else? Would I rather stay home alone and read a good book or just putter? Or none of the above; I want to see what I can find, but I don't need company to do it."

DEVELOPING SELECTIVITY

Just as we are responsible for our own actions, we are responsible for our choice of friends. You, and only you, are responsible for the selection of the people you want to spend time with. Ask yourself: "Am I sure I want this person for a friend? What is the depth of intimacy I am ready for?" If your answer to the first question is positive, you will feel attracted to the other person. You will feel: "I want to know you better. I like you, and I'm interested in you. And I'm going to let you know me."

First impressions can sometimes be misleading. Unfortunately, one of the biggest stumbling blocks in a relationship is judging another by physical standards. The beautiful girl or the handsome man is sought after more often than the plainer counterpart. As we mature, we learn the truth behind many of the old adages. One of those is "Beauty is only skin deep."

The very attractive person sometimes shortchanges herself by not fulfilling her potential in everyday terms, or finding some way she can excel. If she is physically attractive, oftentimes she feels she doesn't have to do anything else. She is already accepted because of her looks.

The first impression you give may signal to others that you are available. That is the signal you want to send to the person who appeals to you, the one you would like to know better. But what about the others? What about people who do not live up to your standards for friends and acquaintances? We've all met people we would rather not count among our acquaintances. There are people whom you are just not interested in knowing. When you meet these people, take the advice of the sixteen-year-old girl: "Walk away." If that's not possible, you can develop signals that say, "I am not interested."

Most of us don't make waves for fear of splashing someone. But you must remember that some people need a little cold water thrown on them now and then. Your "walk away" can be that cold water.

PERSONAL ARMOR

Develop your personal suit of armor. This armor says, "I am not available." If any relationship can exist between us, it must be at arm's length. That is all I am able and/or willing to give you.

Erect your barriers. It is possible to have a congenial association without "friendship." You can create a friendly atmosphere and be pleasant to another person when you have to.

We all have many associations without friendship. There are numerous instances of people having to be together but not by choice—for example, people who work together, play together, go to church together, are a family together, or any other type of together that is formed by something other than choice or selection.

Many of these relationships you should keep at arm's length for your own good.

When you'd rather not be friends, what do you do?

"I don't really do anything to discourage people," says Arlen from Brooklyn. He echoes the most common feeling of how you can deal with those people with whom you'd rather not be friends: "I make myself unavailable."

That's what most people do. Very few people come right out and say: "Go away, I don't like you. I don't want to be friends with you."

The problem of what to do when you'd rather not be friends seems more difficult for younger people than for older ones.

"The older you get, the easier it is," says Madge, an executive in a large firm. "I try to be kind always, to project Christian charity. I discourage people through neglect. That gives me pangs of conscience—until I realize I'm hurting myself. I can't waste my time. I must be selective. After I've given myself this pep talk, I go back to *neglect*—and start all over again."

Neglect is an important part of your personal suit of armor. You must learn to be "removed."

"I don't listen," says a secretary named April. "Everyone knows I have an important job. I have the bosses' ear. I know some people try to cultivate my friendship just because of that. And I resent being used."

There are times when neglect doesn't work. Then what?

NO RESPONSIBILITY

You can be helpful and receptive by listening to the other person, but don't seek advice or comfort from him. Discourage his confidences. If you must listen and respond to that person's confidences, don't permit yourself to get involved emotionally. Above all, don't ask for his advice or comfort. Don't respond in any way to indicate a responsibility on your part. Don't give advice even when asked.

138

Refer the person to a confidential adviser, clergyman, or therapist. If you offer advice, you automatically assume responsibility.

Be wary of the trap. The one seeking friendship will have you ensnared if he can get you to assume any responsibility for him. He will take your advice, and then you will be involved with him emotionally. There's an old Oriental tradition that says when you save another's life, you become responsible for him for the rest of his life. Responsibility is the key word. Once you assume any kind of responsibility for another person, you are linked to that person emotionally.

Paula, a woman over forty, remembers her problem. "When I was in college, there was this fellow in several of my classes. He invited me out many times, but I turned him down. After he asked me out twelve times, I finally gave in just to get it over with, and went out with him." She sighed in remembrance.

"Well, that was the biggest mistake of all. He was dull, stupid, and we had nothing in common. I don't know why on earth I ever accepted that invitation. The only reason was to have a Saturday-night date. That was important in those days. But, by going out with him once, I had encouraged him. I had to say 'No' twenty more times before he stopped calling."

This woman broke the first rule of keeping associates at arm's length: *Be unavailable for outside activities.*

Some people find it more difficult to send out signals that say they are unavailable than the ones that say they are available.

Most of us feel guilty when we send out negative vibrations or signals. Positive ones make us feel good. The neutral level is the hardest to achieve.

"The way I discourage people is by inaction," comments Mike, a busy executive. "I don't smile, talk, touch. I'm curt, brusque, but I'm always polite. I appear distant. I give the impression that I'm in a hurry. I have to be someplace else. This is not calculated behavior. It just happens. The problem is after I have exhibited that kind of behavior, I feel guilty."

Roy, a psychologist, points out: "Guilt can play a big part in getting involved in a friendship you don't want: There are people who practice a kind of emotional blackmail to get you to be a friend. Before you know it, the person will unburden his soul to you with appropriate comments like: 'You're the only one who understands me. You're the only friend I've got. What would I do without you?' That person has unburdened his innermost secrets to you, and you've fallen for the responsibility trap. You've given him advice and helped him do something about his problem. Once you've done that, he has you. You have an emotional stake in his well-being. You are responsible for his action on your advice. You have broken the second rule: *Don't offer advice or comfort."*

"People always ask my opinion," offers Vicki, who works in Connecticut. "I used to give it, because I generally give good advice. Then I learned there was usually more to it than that. People who ask for your advice frequently are asking for more than that. They are asking for a commitment to their well-being. And, although I don't mind giving advice, I do mind being drawn into another's life when I don't want that."

Why do most of us find it harder to give negative signals than positive ones?

Here are five rules to remember when you'd rather not be friends:

RULES FOR KEEPING DISTANCE

1. Be unavailable for outside activities.
2. Don't offer or ask for advice or comfort from the person.
3. Don't permit yourself to get involved emotionally.
4. Don't respond to the person in any way to assume responsibility for him.
5. Don't allow the other person to make you feel guilty.

There are times in our life when we must maintain necessary or obligatory relationships. Sometimes family members are in that category. Relatives are not necessarily friends. We inherit our relatives but acquire our friends. There are family affairs and gatherings where we must spend time with relatives. We establish a congenial relationship. Practice the art of being friendly but not a friend. Be pleasant and decorous in company.

"Be friendly without being a friend." How? The art of being friendly is very much like the art of performing for an audience. No performer could take the time to establish a personal performance for each member of the audience; there would never be time. Yet he can please everyone at the same time with his performance for the whole audience.

Remember the first rule: *Be unavailable for outside activities.* You may give a logical excuse or simply be unavailable. No one is forced to give an explanation. A simple "I'm so sorry I can't make it" will do. What you say is perfectly true. You cannot make it that day because you have something else you'd rather do or someone else you'd rather be with.

SELECTIVITY

Various other relationships in our lives are obligatory and take special handling.

Sigmund Freud pointed out, "The basic requirements of human existence are work and love."

However, we don't always *love* or even *like* some of the people we work with. Yet work is a necessary part of our basic existence. The people we work with are a part of our world. Frequently we spend more time with the people we work with than the people we care about most.

The same rules for congeniality and friendliness with family apply with work associates. Move more slowly with your co-workers, however, since people change jobs much more often than they change relatives.

You are faced with a variety of factors in selecting the people you will spend time with outside of working hours. Which persons will you join on a coffee break? Where will you sit for lunch? Will you go out to lunch with one of your co-workers? Take your time in the workaday world. There are many people you can enjoy on a limited basis. You may want to settle for that until something deeper grows. In the nine-to-five job world people can have motives other than friendship.

Martin, a successful copywriter in New York, relates the story of the time he took a young junior copywriter under his wing. "He was an appealing young fellow, good-looking, friendly, and outgoing. He flattered my ego. He knew I was the best writer in the agency and said he wanted to learn all he could from me. I went out of my way to show him the ropes; even went so far as to give him suggestions on how he could improve his copy. He invited my wife and me to his home for dinner. He improved all right. He improved so much he went to the head of the agency with an idea to take over *my* account. What that so-called *friend* wanted was my job. He tried to use me, and he did—for a while."

Indeed, friends don't use each other for personal gain. Luckily Martin has a strong sense of his own self-worth and could handle the situation with the younger man. For another person the experience might have been more harmful.

"It's the oldest trick in the book," Martin concludes. "When someone turns to you for that kind of guidance and friendship—look out! Nine times out of ten he wants something from you. Now, I ask myself, 'Would that person want me for a friend if I lost my job?' That puts him to the test every time."

SPECIAL ENVIRONMENTS

Other kinds of special environments create necessary relationships. For example, men forge a variety of different group relationships in the armed services. Especially in wartime, this kind of interdependence causes friendships to occur more quickly than under normal circumstances. But most of these relationships are temporary, nonmeaningful on a long-term basis.

Sports teams, amateur or professional, offer a team approach to living as well as playing a game. Being on the team is another type of special environment where you might need the five rules for maintaining distance in your relationships.

Other special environments that create a temporary interdependence are group-travel tours, temporary work units, touring companies, entertainment groups, volunteer organizations, etc. It's easy to establish a temporary friendship; much easier to achieve than the long-term one.

Proximity, in a variety of circumstances, can create this relationship. Frequently it is very close and meaningful at the time, but part of its existence is based on the knowledge that it is temporary, passing, ephemeral. The texture of this relationship is like gauze compared with the long-term friendship, a sturdy wool.

In any situation where you must spend time in close proximity, follow the rules for congenial relationships. Be friendly and enjoy the time together, but be unavailable for additional contact outside the specific environment unless you want the person for a friend. Lay down the ground rules, especially in the male-female friendships. Make sure everyone understands the nature of the relationship. Set boundaries for your own privacy. You have every right to say, "I don't care to go," or "I'd rather not discuss it."

TYPES WHO TAKE ADVANTAGE

The Time Waster

The more successful you become, the more demands on you. Your success can come professionally, financially, creatively, spiri-

142

tually, or in the way you live your life. Successful people are an unwitting magnet that draws others to them. Many of those others are *Time Wasters*. The Time Wasters are people who would take you away from the things you want and need to do or from the people you want to be with.

A favorite trick of the Time Waster is to ask questions. He is almost as good at it as the three-year-old who wants to know the Why? of everything. He will seek your advice but usually not take it.

He's not a happy person and takes a dim view of the world. He's firmly convinced that most other people view the world the same way he does. He's miserable, so he figures everyone else is too.

The Time Waster is a master conversational convoluter. He never says what he means and often talks in circles intentionally or otherwise. While you struggle to make sense out of what he's saying, he has you trapped into listening.

He will discuss anything if you will listen. He needs company and must *kill* time when he is without a specific task or assignment.

Most of us are caught in his trap, because we try to be polite. Few of us have learned to say, "I don't have time for you." Those who have save a great deal of time.

Another one of his favorite tricks is to stand in a position that blocks your way. You literally have to move him to pass by or leave.

Moreover, as we grow and change, friendships change too. Any friendship has to be examined in a realistic light. What are the motives in a friendship? Why is this person friendly now? What does he want? Move slowly until you're sure the other person is being honest. Examine the motives.

There are people who will take advantage of you, whatever the reason.

They will take your time away from the things you would like to do.

Sir Walter Scott wrote:

> Time will rust the sharpest sword,
> Time will consume the strongest cord;
> That which molders hemp and steel,
> Mortal arm and nerve must feel.

Martin, the copywriter, offered his test of a friend. "Would he be my friend if I lost my job?"

Other questions to ask in examining a questionable friendship are:

1. Would this person be my friend if I were broke?
2. Would this person be my friend if I were divorced?
3. Would this person be my friend if I were ill?
4. Would this person be my friend if I were in jail or in a mental hospital?

The Time Waster is concerned with trivial things and will involve you in as many of those trivial things as you will allow. Time for him is something to be filled up, not to make use of. The Time Waster must be firmly discouraged.

There are several other types of people who take advantage where they can. In the following humorous dialogues the types are exaggerated—but only somewhat.

Priscilla the Possessor

PRISCILLA: Oh, I'm so glad you're here.

YOU: You are?

PRISCILLA: Yes, if it weren't for you, I couldn't stay here.

YOU: You couldn't?

PRISCILLA: No way. But you've made it easy. Thank you.

YOU: For what?

PRISCILLA: Just for being here. You know you shouldn't have come. You really don't have the time.

YOU: What are you talking about?

PRISCILLA: We're both playing hooky. Don't you see that gives us a special bond?

YOU: It does?

PRISCILLA: Oh, yes. It means we are a team.

YOU: We are?

PRISCILLA: We are one.

YOU: Now wait a minute.

PRISCILLA: We are responsible for each other. Let's leave this party and go to my house.

YOU: What?

PRISCILLA: I will take care of you.

YOU: You will?

PRISCILLA: Yes, I am responsible for you. I want you all to myself.

YOU: Now, wait a minute.

PRISCILLA: You are mine!

Priscilla is a *Possessor*. She can never get enough of you. These people are jealous of your other friends and frequently put you on

144

the spot with invitations they know you can't accept. They are particularly fond of inviting you for a time when they know you have something else planned. These people want you all to themselves and don't care if there's anything left over for you.

The Possessor is jealous of any of your time spent away from her. She spurs jealousy between friends and sometimes forces you to tell white lies when two friends want you to go someplace with each of them at the same time.

It is very hard to keep the Possessor at arm's length. Once she has established a beachhead of acquaintanceship, which she equates with friendship, she will reinforce it at every opportunity.

Frequently, this person is one who encourages your weaknesses. She knows if you're unhappy with yourself, you'll be more receptive to her. She encourages your feelings of guilt for the same reason.

The only way to operate with the Possessor is to make it very clear that if she wants you for a friend, it must be on your terms. You will not allow her to intrude on your privacy. You will give as much as you are willing to and no more. If she can accept that relationship, fine. If not, you will be unable to continue the relationship on any terms.

Sally the Sponger

SALLY: Can I borrow a safety pin?

YOU: Sure.

SALLY: You just saved my life! I must spend more time with you.

YOU: Well, I'm sure it wasn't your life.

SALLY: Well, almost. Anyway, I want you to know how much I appreciate it. You're absolutely wonderful.

YOU: It was nothing.

SALLY: Wow! That is so like you. You give and give and you don't want any credit.

YOU: For a safety pin?

SALLY: That's just one thing. You're always there with what I need when I need you.

YOU: I am?

SALLY: Yes, I wish I could be more like you. I mean, how you always go out of your way for people all the time. Tell me how you do it.

YOU: Well, I don't always—

SALLY: You must come from an incredible background.

145

You: Well, I—eh—

SALLY: What were your parents like? Where did you grow up? What was it like? Who are the people you care about? Tell me more—More—MORE—

Sally is a *Sponger*. The Sponger is a lot like the Possessor. The Sponger is a person who feels incomplete unless she has another person with her at all times. She will take as much from you as you allow and will continue to soak up your time and energies until you put a stop to it. She is frequently a flatterer and is fond of trapping you into conversations. She is especially fond of the telephone. She manages to keep talking so that you must interrupt to put an end to it. Those people who have been taught that it's impolite to interrupt have the most difficult time terminating a conversation. The more polite you are to this character, the greater advantage she will take.

The Sponger intrudes in your life and makes herself more present than you want or have room for.

She is an incomplete person. The outline is there but no definition. She will be whatever you want her to be as long as she can be with you.

She is literally like a sponge who would soak you up if she could.

Simon the Psychoanalyzer

SIMON: There's something very familiar about you.

You: There is?

SIMON: Yes, I've met you before.

You: Oh, I don't think so.

SIMON: I know your type.

You: You do?

SIMON: Certainly. Don't you realize the way you're standing says you're open to invitations.

You: Huh?

SIMON: The trouble with you is you're too open to strangers. Now if I were your ordinary guy, I might get the wrong idea. But I can tell what you really need is someone who will—sweep you off your feet. Isn't that right?

You: Well, no, not really.

SIMON: Then what is it you do want? What kind of man are you looking for?

You: To tell you the truth I'm not looking.

SIMON: We'll have to change that. Don't you realize you have to start?

You: Start what?

SIMON: Find out why you hate men. Why, with a little work you could be very appealing. Fix your hair, lose a little weight. Take my advice and . . .

Simon is a *Psychoanalyzer*. He knows what's best for you and is only too happy to tell you. The Psychoanalyzer frequently begins a conversation with, "The trouble with you is . . . " or, "What you should do is . . . " or: "Don't you realize why you did that? It's because . . . " He is particularly fond of pointing out your faults and giving you his particular brand of armchair psychoanalysis. He will even interpret your dreams if you'll let him.

He knows what's best for everybody and offers his advice or criticism without being asked.

He fancies himself an amateur psychoanalyst and will make all sorts of suggestions for changing your life: your behavior, your physical appearance, your attitudes, your feelings, etc.

In order to give this free analysis, he asks the most intimate questions about your behavior in all sorts of situations. He is particularly interested in your relationships with other people. He would put you under a microscope if he could. The more you tell him, the more he will offer suggestions for change. He would like to mold you into his ideal image. He thinks of himself as a Henry Higgins and sees you as his Eliza, just like in the musical *My Fair Lady*. He knows you could be perfect if you'd only listen to his ideas on how to make you over.

The only way to handle the Psychoanalyzer is to tell him straight, "Friends don't analyze; friends accept."

Moreover, everyone has secrets and should keep them. Everyone needs a private part of himself that he shares with no one. A person should keep part of himself for himself.

Conrad the Competitor

CONRAD: Want to play?

You: No, thank you.

CONRAD: Come on, everybody plays the game.

You: They do?

CONRAD: Sure. I'll bet I can beat you.

You: I'm sure you can. Let's forget it.

CONRAD: Let's make a bet.

You: I don't want to play.

CONRAD: You're afraid! Because you lost the last time we
   played. Don't you want to avenge your honor?
YOU: All right, Conrad. You're on, I'll play.

(Game begins.)

CONRAD: Ahhh—you cheated!
YOU: What?
CONRAD: You've practiced. You took lessons. You're a pro!
   Foul! Foul!

Conrad is a *Competitor*. He wants to beat you at whatever game
you play. He is only at his best when he can compete with
someone. He devises all sorts of schemes to trap you into competing with him. If he doesn't win, he's angry. And, he will blame you
for his failure. He sees you as responsible for his loss.

He has many excuses for his failure. He will seek out your
weaknesses, and devote any amount of time and energy in that
discovery. Once he has discovered a weakness, he will exploit it.
He doesn't really like you or anybody, but he views you as an
acceptable competitor.

The Competitor will try to manipulate you so that he forces a
competition or contest. He likes a showdown. If he wins, all is well.
He has put you down. But if he loses, he becomes angry and turns
that anger against you. "You cheated! You took unfair advantage."

He'll rant and rave and swear he'll never play you again—until
the next time. Not only will he confront you with these accusations,
but he'll tell anyone who will listen how terrible you are, how you
played the game unfairly, or how you cheated.

In dealing with the Competitor, remember nobody else can hurt
you, only you have the power to let him.

Avoid the Competitor if at all possible. You have nothing to gain
from his acquaintance unless you want to beat him at his own game.

Cora the Collector
   CORA: My dear friend, how are you? You are unique—one of a
      kind.
   YOU: You think so.
   CORA: I know so. You must come to the house on Saturday
      night, dear.
   YOU: Well, I—
   CORA: We're having a party. All our friends, everybody who's
      anybody will be there.

148

You: That's nice.

Cora: You'll be there too, sweet thing. What about your friend Ron? Could you bring him?

You: I don't know. He might be busy.

Cora: Well, you'll bring him to be with us if he's free, won't you? We always have such a good time.

You: Sure.

Cora: Do you think he's really as obnoxious as people say?

You: No, I've never heard—

Cora: What have you heard about him? Tell me all the latest dirt.

Cora is a *Collector.* The Collector has a wide circle of friends and acquaintances. She adds to this circle every chance she gets. She collects people the way some people collect objects. She wants everyone to know you're her friend or acquaintance, although she never uses the word *acquaintance.* Everyone she knows is her *friend.* She frequently uses the pronoun *we* and moves as quickly as possible to a false intimacy. She would have others think you are old and close friends.

She invites you to every party or social gathering she has. It's as if she decorated her house with people. Some of her tactics are like the Possessor's in that she tries to instill the idea that you belong to her in some way. But unlike the Possessor, that sense of belonging to her is only for the benefit of other people. She really doesn't care about you. She talks about people and things but never about ideas.

She is uncomfortable with any conversation other than the most superficial. She loves gossip and will offer choice tidbits about anyone who isn't present or within earshot.

She frequently solicits your opinion about other people and will pass that opinion on to that person discussed if it's in any way derogatory or could be construed as such. She likes to put people together in dramatic confrontation and she precipitates an "incident" whenever possible.

The Collector is more of a pest or nuisance and can be a destructive influence. Therefore, she is a person to be avoided. She will use you for her own viewing pleasure or entertainment with no consideration whatever for your or anyone's feelings.

DISCOURAGING UNWANTED RELATIONSHIPS

"I know I should stay away from characters like the Collector and the Possessor," a young teacher named Jackie says, "but how do I do it? I have to learn to keep people at arm's length or to put them off entirely. But I don't know how. What can I do?"

Jackie's problem is not unique. With so much written and discussed about how to make friends, most people have a lot more information about how to create relationships than how to discourage them. Many people like Jackie need to learn how to say, "No." They need some simple techniques to discourage people from taking advantage of them and creating unwanted relationships.

"I disappear," offers Shirley from Cincinnati. "It's easy to do. If you don't listen, people notice and stop talking to you. Pretty soon they don't care whether you're there or not."

"I don't talk," Sarah offers. "I turn the other cheek, but it's the silent side of me. It's the side that says, 'Hands off.' When I keep my mouth shut, people don't seek me out."

"Sometimes you have to say it," declares a man from Long Island. "You just have to say it. You can soften the message with words like, 'I don't have time for you now,' or 'I'm sorry I'm so busy, but I am.'

"And you can use other people in the room. It's a piggyback ride, but it's one way to get them off *your* back. Steer them to someone else with, 'There's someone over there I want you to meet.' Then walk away after you've introduced them to someone else."

"I'm in such a hurry," offers Margaret from Minneapolis. "That's my favorite line, because most of the time it's true. I don't have time for anyone." She took a deep breath and continued. "Anybody who hangs around me long enough to be a friend is probably someone who is not easily discouraged."

What, then, are the ten ways to discourage others when you'd rather not be friends?

TEN WAYS TO DISCOURAGE OTHERS

1. Don't listen. (When people find you don't listen to them, they go away.)
2. Don't look. (Eye contact is an important way to communicate. When you don't look at the person, it says, "I don't want to see you.")
3. Turn down all their offers.
4. Figure out what they want and offer the opposite.
5. Be in a hurry.
6. Be busy.
7. Don't offer encouragement of any kind.

8. Be supercritical.
9. Bring up a touchy subject.
10. Say, "I don't have time for you."

A twenty-five-year-old sales analyst sums it up this way: "And when you try all ten ways to discourage others, anyone with reasonable intelligence will get the message. But, if he doesn't, you just have to say it. Shake your head and say: 'Go away. I don't want you for a friend.' "

CHAPTER 12

Ending a Friendship

What can you do when a friend changes and the relationship is no longer a happy one? What happens when one person grows and changes, and the other does not? We grow and change at different times on different levels. Sometimes we leave a friend behind or a friend surges forward and is lost to us in our way of life.

Consequently, changes in our lives cause a reassessment of our friendships. In today's mobile society, people move freely from one place or job to another. The person who was your best friend yesterday may be gone tomorrow. In today's world, few of us have the opportunity to know another person well for our whole lives, even in a family. Fewer of us have the opportunity to know friends for a lifetime.

Moreover, geographic relocation can put a graceful end to a friendship. Those relationships which are strong and can withstand the test of time and distance will continue. Actually, a move from one place to another offers a natural hiatus to any relationship. The participants are given a second chance to decide if the friendship is worth keeping. Therefore, the move can be viewed as the natural end of a friendship.

In addition, career changes influence friendship. When one friend is on the rise and the other is headed in the opposite direction, the relationship is bound to change.

CHANGES

Likewise, marriage affects friendship. It is almost impossible for one partner to maintain a friendship with a person whom the husband or wife doesn't like.

What divorce does to a friendship is even more dramatic. Many times friends have to make a choice after the couple splits up. With which partner will they choose to continue their friendship?

One young divorcée named Janice put it this way: "Who gets the friends? Tom and I had no trouble with a settlement. I got the house. He got the car and some stocks. We divided everything else equally. What we couldn't divide was our friends. After the divorce, many of our friends felt they had to choose between us. This is common behavior after a divorce. But it hurt us both. People feel they must take sides and make a decision in favor of the husband or the wife. They think they can remain friends with only one or the other. Oh, there are a few adventurous souls who will try to juggle both. Those friends are always careful of whom they invite when. They make sure never to invite the estranged pair to the same party or the best friend of one, when the other is there."

Although death takes friends from us, the effect we see is on those who are left behind. Frequently there is a profound change in the loved one who must go on without the spouse or dear friend.

Marjorie relates such a problem. "Something has happened to my old friend Ed. He's not the same person he used to be. He doesn't care about himself anymore. He looks sloppy and uses the most outrageous language. I can't listen to his foul mouth. I really don't want him in my home. He seems to have lost more than his wife. I think it's respect for other people, but mainly for himself. He just doesn't care about anything."

Marjorie is a woman who has known her friend Ed since childhood. She and her husband were friends with Ed and his wife for twenty years.

"After Ed's wife died, he changed," Marjorie continues. "We tried to stick by him and share in his grief, but he refused everyone's help. It's as if he didn't want his friends anymore. I don't know what's the matter. He goes out of his way to say things he knows will upset people. I will always care about Ed, but it's better if I end our friendship now while I still have happy memories."

Marjorie had a difficult decision to make. In her case she decided to maintain her memories of the pleasant past with Ed rather than to wait until he did something she could not accept.

Similarly, when our interests and goals change, those changes influence our friendships. When one out of every two marriages ends in divorce, is it any wonder how much change occurs in every relationship, including friendship?

On the other hand, another factor that can influence friendship is—by any other name—money.

Mark Twain put it this way: "The holy passion of Friendship is of so sweet and steady and loyal and enduring a nature that it will last through a whole lifetime, if not asked to lend money."

And he always got a chuckle, but on the other hand, what better way to find out if a friend will support you in your time of need. In addition to money, something more is gained. No one wants to test a friend, but when it happens, it's good to know you can count on that person no matter what; that's an assurance of steadfast loyalty and trustworthiness. The lender sees a trustworthy person; the borrower sees someone who's there when he needs him or her.

"I wasn't happy when I had to borrow one thousand dollars from my friend," says Penny from Pennsylvania. "But I was happy with how fast she answered my need with no questions asked. The affirmation of the friendship was even more important than the money."

Oftentimes, money does cause problems in relationships just as Mark Twain pointed out, but how much more enduring is a friendship that can overcome that problem. That kind of friendship is one between equals.

In fact, a young child thinks nothing of sharing his quarter with a friend. Teenagers share their financial resources more easily than their elders do. The importance of money seems to increase with a person's age.

COMPETITION

Likewise, friendships change at different ages. When you were a child, you played with whoever was available. In school you had a wider choice. Your friends were those who liked to do the same things you did. As you grew and changed, your needs in friendship changed as well. As an adult you forged a friendship with a person with whom you had something in common: common interests, common goals, common dreams for the future. You accepted your friend the way he or she was. And that friend accepted you in the same all-inclusive way. As you grew older, there was less competition in your life and more security.

A friend has a tapestry in her living room that reads: "Competition is for horses, not artists." The saying is credited to Béla Bartók.

"I've been in competition situations with my friends for many years, yet I have never competed with one of them," remarks a

154

public speaker from Ohio. "Let me explain. I was a high school debater and orator. My best friend in high school and I were both in the Prince of Peace oratory contests. Sometimes we spoke on the same programs, but I never felt as though I was in competition against her. We were always competing against everybody else, never each other. Does that make sense?"

Indeed it does. That experience illustrates the saying about competition being for horses and not artists.

"Similarly," our speaker goes on, "when I was in college with another best friend, we were both on the tour as college orators. Again, it was the same way. It didn't matter which one of us took first or who took second, as long as we took both places. We represented our college in competition with the other colleges. I have such fond memories of those days."

How sweet the memories of "friendships past" are. How much has been written about it. How much has been thought about it. It has been a favorite topic among poets down through the ages.

For example, Shakespeare's Sonnet No. 30 offers "remembrance of things past":

> When to the sessions of sweet silent thought
> I summon up remembrance of things past,
> I sigh the lack of many a thing I sought,
> And with old woes new wail my dear time's waste:
> Then can I drown an eye, unus'd to flow,
> For precious friends hid in death's dateless night,
> And weep afresh love's long since cancell'd woe,
> And moan the expense of many a vanish'd sight:
> Then can I grieve at grievances foregone,
> And heavily from woe to woe tell o'er
> The sad account of fore-bemoaned moan,
> Which I new pay as if not paid before.
> But if the while I think on thee, dear friend,
> All losses are restor'd and sorrows end.

OUTGROWING FRIENDSHIPS

After all, some friendships that are no longer meaningful to both parties can be phased out gracefully. It can be done with grace without harshness.

A twenty-five-year-old actor says: "When the time comes, you have to be strong enough within yourself to push people away, so there's no harm done. Give them the hint, and let them take the action. That way you let them save face. You give them the opportunity to walk away."

This young man's career is on the rise. He has very little time for anything or anybody not connected with that career. He has grown and changed but his friends at home have stayed at the same level. He has nothing in common with them anymore. He has outgrown their friendship. They too have moved in different directions.

"When a friendship is over, it simply melts away without any harsh words," explains Dennis from Hawaii. "If it's a real friend, there is an understanding of why it's gone. Often, it slips away from being. Many times there's no blame involved. It just happens. It is simply the time and circumstances of lives at that period in time."

How beautifully put are these words which describe a friendship that's over. The key words are "melts away," "slips away from being," and "circumstances of lives."

With such a relationship as this one, even though it's over, no longer needed or desired, it will be cherished, a happy memory forever.

After all, all of us have certain people in our past we will never forget. At some point in life that person was dramatically *there* when needed. That person may have been the one who enlarged a view of life in some way, or the person we shared an important growing time with.

"I've had two such persons in my life," says Marianne, a biologist. "I don't see either of them much anymore, and it's better that way. But if either of them ever needed anything I could give, I would be there for them in a minute with everything I had. One friend is from college days. We shared the same dreams. She's achieved hers and is now a well-known entertainer. Mine have changed since then. I know if I ever needed anything, especially money, she'd always help me." She stopped for a moment and smiled in fond remembrance.

"My other friend really went out on a limb for me. She literally took me in off the street when I didn't have a place to live. But now her life has changed. It has changed too much. She's been through a lot: a divorce, supported three kids by herself. Life has not been kind to her. She's been hurt and rejected. Consequently, she's grown cynical. I can't blame her, and I probably would have become cynical too in her shoes, but I don't want to be with her now. It hurts me to see her that way. She's changed so much. I'm better off with my 'remembrance of things past.'"

This is one of the hardest relationships to maintain. One person has retained a positive outlook on life, while the other has become negative and communicates those negative feelings.

Consequently, when the goals, the interests, and the ways of looking at life change, there is very little left except the past. The only course to save that past and continue the relationship is to keep the other person in that past at a distance. There can be nothing new or alive in this relationship. It can only be maintained on what it once was. It may phase out naturally in time, even though Marianne says she would do anything for the person if asked. If and when this person did call on Marianne for help, the relationship might be rekindled.

Therefore, each friendship is unique in what you bring to it, and what you take from it. The ideal is to give and take equally, not at the same time necessarily, but over a long period of time.

ACCEPTING CHANGE

"What is critical in a friendship is to accept change," states a college professor named Marvin. "You must be honest with a friend and he with you. You must understand the *grayness* of humanity. Over a period of time, you must accept each other not only as you are but as you change."

Indeed, a problem occurs when one person can accept change and the other cannot.

For example, what can you do when your friend still thinks staying out all night dancing on Saturday night is the only way to have a good time? How do you tell him or her you've changed, you've outgrown the behavior? You're ready for other things, for other experiences, other people. You're ready to move ahead in life.

A forty-year-old artist from Nevada says: "Let the other person in on these changes. Let him know what changes have occurred in you. Tell him about your new interests, your new ways of thinking about things. Tell him about your new goals, what you've done and are doing to achieve those goals. Bring him actively into the changes in your life. He may have changed too, but is afraid to take you into his changes for fear of losing the friendship."

The artist continues: "You don't always have to think alike or even like the same things. But if you retain that mutual respect and admiration for each other, then the friendship can take a lot of growth and change on both your parts."

157

This artist has the right idea. When basic values remain, respect remains too. It's when respect and admiration go out of a friendship that the relationship changes.

"My friend Sally is terrific. She's a pianist and travels a lot giving concerts. Sometimes I don't see her for a year, but we always pick up right where we left off. She's doing things, I'm doing things. We have music in common, but it's more than that. We're both growing and changing. I think we really admire each other as people, in addition to each other's work," a music teacher from Long Island comments.

REMEMBER WHEN?

What can you do when all that's left in a relationship is "Remember when?" Do you remember this or that? You can't continue an association based solely on, Do you remember? After you exchange versions of your memories, what do you have?

After all, friendship should be a constant state of growth. An antonym for the word *grow* is *die*. If a relationship does not grow, it will die. Friendship cannot exist in a vacuum. It is not static. You must bring new things to the relationship. You must nurture it, so you continue to communicate. The level can change; as long as the people do too, all's well.

We create patterns in our lives that work for us. These patterns become habits and take little thought on our part. We learn that action A usually provides result B, and that action C results in goal D. As we grow and change, sometimes we forget to change our patterns or at least reexamine them This examination helps us ensure our own growth and direction. However, we must experiment with new combinations. We are no longer the same person we were when we first devised those patterns.

Even Paul said, "I do not understand my own actions."

We all go through many changes in our lives. Like Paul we don't always know why we do certain things at specific times. But we do know we change. Life experiences dictate changes.

Sometimes our loyalty to an old friend can actually be detrimental to ourselves. It can be hazardous to our own survival. When this happens our patterns of behavior must be examined carefully. Take Bob, for example. If he didn't change his old behavior, it would be hazardous to his health.

158

DIALOGUE 1

GEORGE: Let's go to O'Neil's to watch the ball game, like old times.

BOB: I'd rather go someplace else tonight.

GEORGE: But it's Thursday. We always used to watch the ball game at O'Neil's on Thursdays.

BOB: How about bowling?

GEORGE: Bowling? What's the matter with you? We'll have a few beers, a few laughs, just like we always did.

BOB: I don't drink anymore.

GEORGE: Aw, come on. A coupla beers won't hurt ya. Some of the old gang will be there—I told them you were in town—like old times.

BOB: No, thanks, George. I'd better not.

GEORGE: What's the matter—too good for your old friends since you moved away?

BOB: No, George, the matter is—I'm an alcoholic. I stay out of bars nowadays.

Habits change. People change. Loyalties change also. We must learn to deal with a relationship where it exists in this moment in time, not where it once was.

In the next dialogue, just as in the first one, you can see the problem that exists in the *now* of the relationship.

DIALOGUE 2

GLORIA: Hey, Debbie, long time no see. You look wonderful, but then you always were a good-lookir' kid since I can remember.

DEBBIE: Thanks! You look great too. How long has it been?

GLORIA: How long? Let's see. You left here the year of my first divorce. That would be four years ago last March.

DEBBIE: Your first divorce?

GLORIA: Yeah, I'm workin' on my third one right now.

DEBBIE: Third divorce?

GLORIA: Yeah, how about celebrating with me? Like old times, remember?

DEBBIE: I remember. Every time you broke up with a guy, we'd go out and pick up a couple new ones.

159

GLORIA: What's a best friend for? You were always there. Well, what do you say? There's a new roller disco in town, lots of action.

DEBBIE: How about dinner at my mom's place? She's expecting me.

GLORIA: Are you kidding? With three strikes on me, I gotta go right back up to bat, so I don't freeze the next time. Come on.

DEBBIE: I'm married now, Gloria.

GLORIA: So where is he?

DEBBIE: He's back in Philly. I came out alone to see Mom.

GLORIA: So, what he doesn't know won't hurt him. Come on, we'll kick up our heels a little. You probably need it as much as I do.

DEBBIE: Maybe some other time, Gloria.

GLORIA: But, I need you now.

DEBBIE: I'm sorry, Gloria, but I don't need you. Better luck next time!

On the other hand, "I cherish survivors," a thirty-nine-year-old woman from New York says. "In this town you have to be one. I am attracted to people who have survived, to the ones I know are survivors. I am just beginning to learn how to be a survivor myself. I used to let a blind sense of loyalty get in my way. I cared more about other people's survival than I did my own."

She stopped for a moment in an effort to understand her own behavior. "Since I've married, my life is turned around. I have no friends from my past, because I was a different person then. I was passive. All my relationships were the dominant-passive kind. I was always the underdog. My friends back then were all malcontents. I did a lot of analyzing and taking care of them. My maternal side got a good workout. None of those people are a part of my life now. Then I was pretending to be someone else. Now I am accepted for who I am—not the role I play. My husband helped me find the person I really am. It's my first relationship of equals."

BLIND LOYALTY

Although loyalty is the most desired quality in a friendship, blind loyalty can create problems. Chapter 4 pointed out that loyalty was the one quality in a friendship people valued most. What happens when loyalty smacks squarely up against survival?

What do you do when your loyalty is betrayed? It's one thing when a friend lets you down or doesn't live up to the standards set, but what of the person who deliberately sets out to betray you? Or the friend who sets out to test your loyalty and accuses you of betrayal in a friendship?

Some people operate on the "all or nothing" principle. They must continually test the fiber of a relationship.

Sarah was such a person. Sarah needed absolute proof that her friend Georgia was loyal to her. She knew Georgia had saved a thousand dollars for her vacation, so Sarah asked to borrow the thousand dollars. Georgia was surprised at her friend's need and wondered if it were genuine, but offered a compromise.

"You can have five hundred dollars," Georgia said. "That's half of my savings. I'll split it with you."

Sarah saw this as a breach of loyalty. She felt in a true friendship there should be no limits or boundaries. She was not willing to accept the compromise.

"If you were a true friend and loyal to me, you would lend me the whole thousand dollars," Sarah said.

Georgia tried hard to explain to Sarah how she felt. Friendship must be a compromise. But Sarah would have none of it, she felt betrayed.

Pentimento, the book by Lillian Hellman, later the film *Julia,* deals with loyalty and the testing of a friendship. It examines how strong the bond of friendship can be across divided and distinguished worlds.

FATAL BLOWS

Sometimes people let you down once too often or too hard. When that happens, loyalty must be reexamined. As George Santayana said, "Those who cannot remember the past are condemned to repeat it."

Only a fool will let loyalty to an old friend from the past overcome several negative experiences. If and when that time comes, make a clear break. Have you thought about the times when a friend is probably taking advantage of you?

1. Continually borrowing money and never paying you back.
2. Asking for favors all the time but too busy when you need a favor.
3. Wanting you to introduce him or her to all the eligibles of the opposite sex but never doing the same for you.

4. Needing your sympathy and listening ear often but never having time for you.
5. Accepting your every invitation but never inviting you anyplace.
6. Picking your brain for ideas and advice but never having any thoughts to share.

Similarly, there are times when people behave in unacceptable ways. We all set our own boundaries for what is acceptable to us.

However, when someone's behavior out of fear or guilt results in harm to you or to others, or when blame is put on you in order to save the others, this is unacceptable behavior.

Ambition and power can play strange tricks on people as well as their friendships.

Furthermore, some people kill a friendship by doing something so terrible that you can no longer forgive and forget. When this happens, it's time to make a clean break and walk away.

The ambitious person who cares more about his rise to success than he does about people will often use anyone he can. Again, when the pattern is repeated, it's time to break.

Alex, a young lawyer with a prestigious law firm, was having dinner with his boss in a fine restaurant in Philadelphia. An old school friend, who had been disfigured as a child, came over to greet him. Alex barely gave a perceptible nod and did not introduce him to his boss. What Alex never knew was that his school friend was a well-known, highly respected partner of a law firm his boss esteemed very highly. The boss had second thoughts about Alex. The school friend wrote Alex off as a friend he no longer needed or wanted.

Ambition can bring about strange behavior patterns. Ambition is frequently linked with power, which is frequently linked with gold.

"In prosperity our friends know us; in adversity we know our friends." (John Churton Collins.)

How many business partnerships have gone down over money disputes. One only needs to read about a sensational divorce case to see what an important part money can play in dissolving a relationship.

How often are certain familial ties held tightly by threat of disinheritance.

Yes, just as the lust for gold can affect all human relationships, friendship is not exempt from its effects.

Betrayal is present in many human relationships. Nevertheless, why are so many of us loath to accept the evidence when a friend betrays us? We don't want to believe our friends would let us down. And yet there comes a time in everyone's life when he must open his eyes and face the truth: "Not everyone stays a friend forever." Which one of the following friendships would you phase out?

1. You're missing your new gold watch. Your friend George is the only one who was in your apartment. This is not the first time something is missing after George has been there.
2. Your friend told your husband about your escapades in the singles scene before you were married, and insinuates you still do a little running around when he's out of town. This friend has caused trouble in your marriage before.
3. This friend criticizes you in public every chance she gets and ridicules you in private to anyone who will listen. When confronted, she denies saying anything and questions your loyalty as a friend.

Each one of these people gives ample grounds for terminating the friendship. Unless there are unusual or mitigating circumstances, none of these people is a friend worth keeping.

Ending a friendship calls for the same techniques as discouraging friendship, only more so. The difference is that ending a friendship is harder because there once was a relationship that is no longer there. Too often we continue on the basis of what "was" rather than what "is." We remember things the way they used to be rather than the way they are. Take a good long look at the relationships in your life. Are they valid today?

People must find continuous signs of encouragement in a friendship; if there's no reinforcement, it's understood the relationship is no longer there.

If words are called for, tell the truth. Be kind, but tell the truth. Don't try to color the truth. It will only make it harder. Tell the truth and walk away.

It's still the best way to end a friendship that's over—Walk away.

CHAPTER 13

Friendship: The Working Relationship

Luck plays a large part in finding friends, and working on the relationship plays a larger part in keeping them. Often there is an attraction between two persons that cannot be explained in any rational manner. Many people credit chance or luck. "Just be at the right place at the right time. That's the single most important factor in finding friends," so some folks say.

There is a difference of opinion on this assumption, however. One person feels he has to seek out friends. Another disagrees and argues she can't consciously look for friends. Still another thinks friendship either occurs or it doesn't.

"You search for gold or buried treasure but not for friends. When you find a friend, it's plain old-fashioned luck." That opinion is from a saleswoman in Boston.

The manager in the same store offers his feelings: "Sometimes I do seek out friends. When I come across a potential friend, it's a happy pairing of congenialities, but there's some luck involved. A friend is really hard to define. Once you have one, you know it."

When you find a friend or someone you'd like for a friend, what are the ways you can promote the growth of that friendship?

PROMOTING GROWTH

Chapter 6 pointed out ways to promote friendship and bridge the gap from acquaintance to friend. Some of those same elements promote the growth of friendship.

Certainly the first one, *Be in proximity,* is important for any growing relationship. *Respect each other* is another way to promote

164

the growth of friendship. These additional elements are important too in promoting the growth of a working friendship:

Show sincere interest.
Talk together.
Listen to each other.

For the working friendship, another element is necessary, the element of support. The last rule then is, *Be supportive.* We've all met people who are supportive. Those people encourage you in whatever ways you need. They believe in you. They believe in your growth.

Sarah is an architect and a supportive friend. She is always there for a friend when needed. Not on a regular basis perhaps; but when someone needs a point of view, an opinion, or a critical eye on an important work, Sarah will be there. Moreover, Sarah will always give an honest evaluation when asked.

"My comments are not always popular," Sarah says. "But, if I'm going to be a supportive friend, I must give an honest opinion. I can always commend the effort if not the results. We all have to go back to the drawing board now and then. I figure it's better if I point out a mistake than have a friend discover it when it's a million-dollar job for a client who won't offer a second chance."

Supportive friends have an obligation not only to be there for a friend but to offer an honest opinion when asked. Remember the old line: "If your best friend won't tell you, who will?"

"What should a friend do? What is my obligation in a friendship? What are some of the ways I can help it grow and be supportive of my friend?" These are questions people ask themselves over and over again. In friendly relationships, each person continuously grows. Each one brings new things to that friendship. There is an effort on both parts to accept the person as he is.

"My friend offers me security. He's a stabilizing influence, and he never takes sides. Even though we have little in common, he is always supportive of me," offers a forty-year-old industrialist.

What are some ways people "work" at making friendships grow? A group of college students answered the question this way:

"Do favors without being asked."
"Do favors without expecting anything in return."
"I lead an interesting life and I share it with my friends."
"I like to share a conversation with my friend."
"Touch a friend, both physically and mentally."
"Be yourself in accepting a friendship. Be the person you are."

"Bring new things to the friendship, activities, ideas, etc."
"Know when your friend hurts and be there for him."
"Be sensitive to the things that involve the other person. (Don't be self-centered.)"
"Plan things for the other person. (Surprise her sometimes.)"
"Let him know you believe in him."
"Enlarge her view of life or her appreciation for life."

Ways to help friendship grow need not be complicated or earth-shattering—just a small thing that says, "I care." Send a card; call and say "Happy Birthday," or "I was thinking about you, so I thought I'd say 'Hello.'" Tell your friend you appreciated something she did. Learn to give feedback of a positive and negative nature. Know when and when not to speak up with that feedback.

POSITIVE SUPPORT

"What do you think?" is a question that can be a positive booby trap if you let it.

One actress from New York who has been to hundreds of opening nights throughout the country to see friends in all kinds of plays has worked out some carefully worded phrases in answer to that question. She uses these phrases at times when a noncommittal comment is called for.

"There are times when you want to say something without hurting anyone's feelings, especially when the play was dreadful!" the actress admits. "After all, what you really want to say is, 'I loved you, but hated the role,' or 'I loved you but hated the play or the whole production.' But no one in the theatre wants to hear that, especially on opening night. She wants some kind of compliment or commendation on her work. We all do!"

She paused for a moment and then added confidentially, "It's taken me years to come up with 'a line for every occasion,' but I will share a few of them with you."

Here are three lines the actress offers as her noncommittal, supportive comments:

"You've done it again!"
"What can I say!"

And perhaps the most honest one of all which bears no connection with the work is:

"You're wonderful!"

166

Indeed, a friend learns how to say what the other person wants to hear, not all the time, but those special times when it's necessary. A friend tries to empathize and feel for the other person. There are times when the white lie is needed.

WALK-A-MILE

One positive way to help friendships grow is to learn how to put yourself in the other person's shoes. For example, try the role-play game called Walk-A-Mile. The title comes from an American Indian saying: "Don't judge any man until you have walked two moons in his moccasins."

Young children play this game all the time without knowing it. They try on their mother's shoes or dress and hat, their father's jacket or gloves. It's not "dress up" to them. They *are* mother or father. Many a parent is shocked to hear his own words come from a child's mouth when the child assumes the parental role.

Maybe you've heard:

"I'm too busy to do that now."
"I can't do it *all* by myself."
"Do you think I'm made of money?"
"Will you hurry up! I spend half my life waiting for you."

Most parents have said some of those lines and heard them repeated from their children as part of their role-play games.

Now it's your turn for a role-play exercise. Try the Walk-A-Mile game. You can do it alone or play it like charades, with one or more friends.

Select the person you will be (whose moccasins you will walk-a-mile in); the person you will role-play. Take an article of clothing the person usually wears. (It doesn't have to belong to him, just a facsimile of the clothing.) If he always wears a cap or a scarf, use one of those things as your article of clothing. You can use an object also. For example, if that person always has a pencil behind his ear or a paintbrush or hammer in his hand, use one of those things as your object. He may have a particular object associated with his profession, for example, a stethoscope for a doctor, a piece of chalk for a teacher, or a whistle for an athletic coach.

Think about the person for a few minutes. Does he have a particular walk or movement that characterizes him? Does he hold his head in a certain position, or have a characteristic gesture with his hand? What about his speaking voice? Is it very high-pitched?

167

Does his speech have a rhythm pattern or does he use certain words frequently? Speak aloud as that person. (Don't be bashful.) Try introducing yourself as that person: "Hello, my name is Otto. I'm a carpenter from the South."

What else is there about that person that sets him apart from others? Does he laugh a lot? Chew on a toothpick? Hitch up his pants? Does she smooth down her hair or flip her head back in a certain way? Try introducing yourself again and add the characteristic gesture.

In a play script it would look like this:

> You: (*with a Southern drawl*) How do you do. My name is Otto. (*Hitches up pants*) I'm the carpenter here. (*Takes toothpick from pocket and chews*)

Remember, you have three elements "of identification" for your person in your role play: an article of clothing or an object, something vocally in the way he speaks, and one other physical or personality characteristic.

Use all three things together. Speak, move, and touch your object. Now comes the important part. Say something about the way he feels as you think he would. If you're playing the game with friends, talk about something you've heard someone express an opinion on. If it happens to be an opinion you disagree with, all the better.

One role-play soliloquy might sound like this:

> "I think there should be more welfare. Why should anyone have to work? After all, the government should take care of its people."

That's a particularly difficult speech for this conservative Republican from Ohio who is doing the role-play exercise.

Of course, the object of the game played this way is to see if the other members of the group can guess what person you are role-playing—whose moccasins did you choose to walk-a-mile in. This can be a very revealing and insightful game.

Set a time limit of two or three minutes for your verbalizing or soliloquy as the person. Then ask your friends if they can guess who you were in the role play.

Here's another example:

> "I just want to tell you how bad your child is in school. He talks all the time, is loud and unruly, and has no respect for the

teacher. In fact, Mrs. Jones, I have to wonder what kind of home he comes from."

The last line is said with pursed lips, folded arms, and feet planted squarely apart.

Everyone guessed that this portrayed a teacher in the local school. Several of the parents had problems with her at various times.

You can also do this exercise by yourself.

If you are doing it for your own benefit, use a mirror to help you. Speak to the "you" in the mirror as the person you are role-playing.

This can be especially helpful if you've had an argument or a misunderstanding with the person you've chosen to role-play. Keep in mind that you are trying to understand the situation from the other person's point of view. What you are doing in order to understand the other person is putting yourself in his shoes—just as the saying advises: "Don't judge any man until you have walked two moons in his moccasins."

One friend tried the exercise after a misunderstanding on carpool responsibilities.

"You always drive on Friday. Whatever made you think I was going to drive today? We traded days last week, but we weren't supposed to this week. Don't you remember, I said I didn't have to trade, but you said it would be better if we kept it—Uh-oh!"

This woman realized a simple error when she put herself in her friend's shoes.

ROLE PLAY

Perhaps you'd like to try the game first with a specific fictional role to play. Find an article of clothing or object that you associate with a particular character-type you choose for your role-play dialogue. The object is an important part of the role play for you. It will give you a tangible article upon which to concentrate. That focused concentration will help you forget about yourself.

Select one or more of the following roles to do alone in front of your mirror. Once you have tried several, you might want to tape record some for yourself. Listen to the dialogue as if you are listening to another person. (Don't forget you *are* the other person; you're playing another role.)

Role Play 1

You are a very shy person. Your friend has just said something to you that questioned your loyalty in the friendship. You are hurt and angry. You have always been loyal. Explain to your friend how you feel.

This soliloquy might go something like this. Look at this for an example but make up one of your own.

> "You really hurt me when you said I didn't care about you. I do, I care a lot, but I can't always say it. I do lots of things for you to show it. I'm probably the most loyal friend you have, I always stick up for you. I feel lots of things, but it's hard for me to talk about that, I'm too shy. I feel awful. You hurt me a lot."

Role Play 2

You are friendly and outgoing. Your best friend is very sensitive but also very friendly with everyone. Lately she's been extremely friendly to your husband. You think your husband misunderstands her advances. Explain to her, in a nice way, that her actions are easily misunderstood by the opposite sex.

Here is an example of how this soliloquy might go.

> "Listen, Genevieve, I know you're a very friendly, outgoing person, but sometimes people misunderstand your friendliness. Especially men. They don't always realize that you're kidding when you come on the way you do. Sometimes, it sounds as though you really mean it. Take my husband, Ralph, for instance, he knows you, but—even he wonders sometimes. I just thought I'd let you know. Maybe you ought to cool it for a while. Try to be more friendly to the wives the next time there's a party."

You're on your own with the next two. See what you can do with role plays 3 and 4.

Role Play 3

You are a dynamic, aggressive businessman. You don't have time for many friends outside of business. You'd like to know a colleague better. Invite him to join you for a nonwork-oriented activity. Don't take "No" for an answer.

Role Play 4

An appealing person has extended an invitation for dinner to you. You are overwhelmed by work and family problems. You have very

170

little time for anything else. But this is a person you would like to know, a potential friend. Reject the invitation in such a way to let the person know you are rejecting the invitation and not the person.

How did you do on these?

Why not go back and try the role-play situations again from a different point of view? Try them from the person's role you were talking to.

NURTURING A FRIENDSHIP

Indeed, there are many aspects of ourselves we learn through our friend's eyes. The way a friend thinks of us can change our way of thinking about ourselves. Those perceptions are important to us. We need to give and receive feedback. In order to keep a friendship going, it takes special nurturing.

For example, several professional people were asked the question: "What qualities do you bring to maintain a friendship?"

Myra, a thirty-five-year-old college professor, answers this way: "I'm a good listener. I've had a lot of ups and downs with life's problems. I bring that to a friendship. I give good advice.

"I'm a kind of security system. I try to lead my friends through to their own best decision. I've lived a lot and learned a lot through living. I bring that to a relationship. It helps me to see things clearly for other people—sometimes more clearly than I see things for myself.

"I'll always be there for my friends. And if I can do a favor, I always try. I go out of my way for people."

Mildred, an executive in a cable television company, has another answer: "I bring an openness, an affection. I'm not afraid to show affection and/or accept it. And, I don't even resent friends lying, if it has to do with hurt feelings."

"I try to exude those qualities I expect from other people," remarks Harvey from Illinois.

"What I bring to a friendship is passion, integrity, honesty, stubbornness, and a sense of responsibility," states Mitchell, a film director. "Plus intelligence, insight, and excitement."

Harry from Iowa explains: "I bring complete honesty. Sometimes it's too much honesty. I'm an open book. I can be overbearing in my desire to help someone. It can be a burden—for both of us."

"I respect a confidence. In fact, I'd rather die than tell something I was told in confidence. And, I'm a good listener. I really listen to

171

people. I am nonjudgmental. I accept my friends with all their quirks." This is from a lighting designer named Ivan.

A children's theatre director from New York says: "I support my friends. I try to fulfill the needs of the other person: business needs, social needs. I would go out of my way to see that the person's needs were met. I support people when they need that—when I'm in a position to support them. On important issues I really go all out to help."

"I bring fun and humor," says a fifty-year-old playwright named Charlene. "I am also loyal . . . sometimes beyond the point of good sense, and I accept a friend just the way he or she is. I think one of the most important qualities I bring to a friendship is the belief in my friends. I often have confidence in their abilities that they don't have themselves. One of the ways I nurture a friendship is by sharing my joy of living."

LIMITED FRIENDSHIPS

Although friendships should be freely given and freely received, there are times when we give more than we receive. The reverse is true also. At other times we take more than we can give.

On occasion we offer friendship in one area but not in another. We will play tennis with a friend but not talk about our latest adventure in life. We can talk shop with another person, but don't talk about our family with him. We have different friends for different reasons. Limited friendships serve a positive purpose in our lives.

People who are like-minded offer one level of friendship; others who think very differently from the way we do offer a different kind of relationship. Men seem to enjoy "doing" relationships more often than women. Men have friends for golf, for going to the fights, for watching football at the local club or bar. These friendships are limited, and both parties know it. Usually, neither one wants the relationship to be any more than it is. Each person realizes the other's differences and accepts them. The two can be friends on one level but not on another. They choose to keep their friendship from going past the fourth level: *someone to share mutual experiences and special times with.* Yet both value this friendship even with its limitations.

Do women have more friendships than men? It would seem so. Women have been brought up to reach out more freely than men. They instigate more relationships and invest the time and energy to nurture those relationships. Most women have no trouble forming a limited relationship rather quickly. They seem to feel a commonality in the very fact that they are women. They share many physical similarities and go through the same body changes as they mature. Any woman who has given birth shares that experience with every other woman who has had a child. Wives and mothers immediately have a common meeting ground, a place to begin.

Men rarely use the fact of being a husband and a father as the common denominator for friendship. They are much more likely to begin a relationship on work, sports, or some kind of "doing" association. And they use location or being a neighbor to begin a limited friendship.

Furthermore, many limited friendships occur for specific reasons. Frequently a limited friendship is the only way the friendship could last.

Dorothy, an outgoing woman in New York, says: "I find friends in the strangest places. I make friends with the busboy in a restaurant, an elevator operator in an office building I visit frequently, the matron in the ladies' room. All these people are my friends. Granted, all these relationships are momentary and on a limited basis, but I enjoy all of them. Those limited friendships are important to me."

On the other hand, another kind of limited friendship is described. "My best friend moved away several years ago. Her husband is a very prominent lawyer now. His reputation is worldwide. They move in different circles, both economically and socially. The fact that we live in different places is really what has allowed our friendship to continue on the sixth level. My husband and I go to visit them once or twice a year. They are always too busy to visit us, but that's all right. I understand and don't even question. But my friend and I keep in touch by phone or letters. We can always pick up where we left off. We still have the same basic values and cares and can discuss anything. We are nonjudgmental and accept each other totally. But, I know if we still lived in the same town, it would be much harder to maintain that level of intimacy, because the difference in our life-styles would be too obvious," a housewife in Pennsylvania comments.

"What about cross-generational friendships? Those are in the limited category and rightly so," adds an editorial assistant in New Jersey. "I've kept in touch with my high school English teacher for the past six years, and I intend to continue that relationship as long as I can. She's the one who really encouraged me in my writing.

That's a relationship I cherish and value very highly. We never were best friends or neighbors and neither of us would want that. Yet ours is a very special relationship. It moved from the teacher-student level to a friendship between colleagues or equals. She made that happen. She started treating me like an equal which opened the door for me to do the same. We both love many of the same things and share an exciting life of the mind. This is a limited friendship that I will work very hard to maintain."

Many doctor-patient relationships fall into this category. Perhaps more are on the limited association level than limited friendship. Certainly the therapist-patient relationship does, and oftentimes the clergyman-congregation member, lawyer-client, and the professor-student.

In fact, there are many valuable types of limited friendships. These are important in everyone's life. Some people do not have time for any other kind of friendship but the limited one. Some people have created barriers to protect themselves because of a change in their life situations. They can only accept friendship on a limited basis.

Other people prefer the limited-basis friendship. Consequently, if you want that person for a friend, you "take it or leave it" on the limited basis.

Nevertheless, don't overlook the benefits of the limited friendship.

Many relationships serve both parties well without reaching the level of intimacy. In fact, if a level of intimacy is reached in such a relationship, it can ruin it.

As Seneca said, "Friendship always benefits; love sometimes injures."

Harold, a young executive with an international company, says: "There are times in my life when I can't accept anyone's friendship. The things going on in my life are just too all-consuming and pressing for my immediate attention. When someone reaches out to me during this period, it's no good no matter who he is. 'I can't be your friend right now,' is what I want to say. 'I don't have time. Come back another time.' But I don't say anything, I just turn on the cold shoulder. It's simpler that way."

"I can only give what I have time for. And I won't take any kind of friendship unless I have time to give something back," affirms Armond, a busy television executive.

Moreover, there are people who prefer all their relationships on a limited basis. In that way, they don't invest themselves with any one person. They are free for a large variety of acquaintances or limited friendships.

LONG-DISTANCE FRIENDSHIPS

On the other hand, some limited friendships occur because of actual geographical distance.

If the relationship is a solid one, both parties can usually pick up where they left off. But time and location have an effect. Interests change, goals change, loyalties shift. People's needs and desires take a turn in another direction.

What are some ways to nourish and maintain a long-distance friendship?

One person has to make an effort to keep the relationship going. It can be the once-a-year phone call, a birthday card, the call from a mutual friend with your greetings when he's passing through, a postcard, a note with only a few words.

No friendship can be totally one-sided. There must be some reciprocity. If you make the effort to keep in touch, you expect the other person to acknowledge that effort in some way.

Two college friends went their separate ways in different parts of the country. For several years they saw each other two or three times a year and corresponded half a dozen times. Finally, the communication dwindled down to nothing. Neither had heard from the other for over a year. Finally, Paula decided to break the ice. She sent a postcard to her friend, Shirley, with one word on it: "DEAD?" Shirley answered the postcard in like manner. Her postcard read: "NO!"

But communication was reestablished, and they both enjoyed the humor of the cards. Shirley wrote a long letter and brought Paula up to date on her hectic life.

"You keep the relationship going via long distance," a young doctor in Philadelphia affirms. "Actually, my best friend is better at it than I am. He's the one who keeps the ball rolling. When he moved to California, he said he'd keep in touch and he does. He keeps me posted on his life, his family happenings. Even the dog."

Maxim Gorky said about Tolstoy, "As long as he is alive I am not alone."

Friends understand when you can't see them. When you do, the quality of time together is rich. So, remember the good times. Relive the important days. The long-distance relationships can survive on past situations.

A forty-eight-year-old writer named Nathan offers this advice: "Intellectual honesty is the basis for my friendships, whether they are in the working relationship stage, a limited friendship, or maintaining the long-distance one. That's what counts. I want someone I can learn from and teach something to, someone who will share adventure of any type, physical or mental. Distance really has nothing to do with it."

Therefore, maintaining a limited friendship (including the long-distance one) takes a certain amount of skill. As in most relationships, just the right word at the right time often makes the difference in whether the relationship continues and becomes a vital ingredient in your life or whether it withers and dies. It's up to you to decide which way you want it to go. A little practice in finding the right words at the right time can help you set the direction for the relationship.

Here are three dialogues. Each of them has three possible next lines. Choose the line you would say if you wanted to continue the relationship.

DIALOGUE 1

BOB: You'll never believe what just happened.
TOM: What?
BOB: I saw your wife out to lunch with her boss.
TOM: So? He's her boss.
BOB: It didn't look like business to me!
TOM: What did it look like?
BOB: Do I have to draw you a picture?
TOM: Well, just exactly what were they doing?
BOB: They were . . . Well, you know, . . . very chummy.
TOM: (*Choose your line.*)
    (1) Mind your own business!
    (2) Things aren't always what they seem. Forget about it.
    (3) You're a liar and a troublemaker, and I don't believe a word of it.

DIALOGUE 2

DONNA: I have two complimentary tickets for the concert tonight at Lincoln Center. Would you like to go?
JENNY: Oh, I'd love to. I really would, but I can't.
DONNA: Why not?

176

JENNY: I just can't, that's all.
DONNA: That's not a reason.
JENNY: It's personal.
DONNA: Is it me?
JENNY: Of course it's not you.
DONNA: Well, then, tell me why you can't go.
JENNY: (*Choose your line.*)

    (1) It's none of your business.
    (2) I can't go with you this time. That's all there is to it, but please ask me again.
    (3) I don't want to go anyplace with you *ever*!

DIALOGUE 3

JOHN: I hear one of us is going to be the new assistant manager.
MARSHA: So I hear. The boss has narrowed down his choice to one of us.
JOHN: I think he's smart enough to choose the right one.
MARSHA: I hope so.
JOHN: Do you have any doubts?
MARSHA: What do you mean?
JOHN: I want that job and I'm going to get it.
MARSHA: I want it too.
JOHN: This is a man's job. You're not smart enough to handle it!
MARSHA: (*Choose your line.*)

    (1) That's what you think. I'll show you.
    (2) You're entitled to your opinion even if it is different from mine.
    (3) Oh, yeah! I'll show you, you male chauvinist pig!

In each of the dialogues, line 2 is the best choice if you want to continue the relationship.

Answer 1 is probably the most common reaction to the situation and will not damage or encourage the relationship. Choice 3, signals loud and clear that you want no further discussion and/or association with that person.

Remember that earlier in the book friendship was likened to a garden. You must plant a seed in the right environment, if the conditions are right, the seed will grow. All plants need tending just as friendships do. They need care. Any gardener knows how much time, effort, and energy goes into nurturing a garden.

Consequently, you must decide where your major efforts will go. Is it easier to tend one or two special plants carefully and give the others less time and effort? Sometimes the area needs weeding, so the right plants can grow and not be strangled by the heartier weeds. Not all plants bloom, nor do friendships. And, we wouldn't want them to. But there is room in your garden for other plants that serve their purpose.

On the other hand, many sturdier plants offer variety in a garden and take less time, energy, and responsibility. They help to enrich the soil and add color to the overall picture. It's up to you which kind of garden you want, which kind of friendship.

You may find various types of friendship at different times in your life. Be receptive to each. And remember—friendship is a *working relationship*.

CHAPTER 14

Lasting Friendships

Why do some friendships last forever? What is it about the bond of friendship that makes it unique?

Most answers to this question are more emotional than rational. True friendships have a certain nonverbal communication understood between two persons.

Remember how Cicero defined friendships? "A complete accord on all subjects human and divine, joined with mutual good will and affection."

He commented further on lasting friendships with these words: "Only those are to be judged friendships in which the characters have been strengthened and matured by age."

In other words, only a long-term friendship can be judged a true friendship.

Moreover, Montaigne says a perfect friendship is possible only with *one* other. "This friendship that possesses the soul and rules it with absolute sovereignty cannot possibly be double. . . . A singular dominant friendship dissolves all other obligations. The secret I have sworn to reveal to no other man, I can impart without perjury to the one who is not another man, *he is myself.*"

Montaigne sees this perfect harmony of two individuals coming together as one. Indeed, he thinks of his friend and himself as one person. "In the friendship I speak of, our souls mingle and blend with each other so completely that they efface the seam that joined them, and cannot find it again."

The long-term or lasting friendship is very special and holds a very special place in literature, history, and our own hearts.

Yet is this something special always the same quality? Is it a coming together in spirit so completely that friends become *one* and the seam can no longer be found?

MEANINGS OF FRIENDSHIP

How do friends today describe the elusive meaning of friendship? Here's how a thirty-eight-year-old artist describes the meaning of friendship in his life. "It's a glow. You feel it. You accept the other person's differences. You love the essence of that person."

"For me I have to have more than one person," declares a theatre teacher named Marsha. "I know friends I haven't seen in years, yet I know they're there. Once I wondered what I liked about people. I made a list, and it was a strange list. All the people on it were so different. I couldn't figure out what the common thing was that I liked about them.

"I finally figured it out. I liked their soul or their spirit. The spirit was the same no matter what their education, background, financial status, social position, etc. There was a love shining through. That's the quality I find in friendships that last."

She went on to say: "That's why I like children. That spirit hasn't been covered up or glossed over yet. I get excited about that spirit."

Still, the friendship bond is unique—open-ended. It has a tolerance for growth and change. We stand the best chance of being ourselves with friends. You don't have to put your best foot forward or put on a happy face. You can just BE. And, you can be the way you are and the way you want to be.

FRIENDSHIP PROCESS

Furthermore, friendship can be viewed as a process rather than a product. It is an ongoing state never complete, never finished, in which both parties continue to contribute, grow, and change.

Henry Adams said, "One friend in a lifetime is much; two are many; three are hardly possible."

Yet some people create solid friendships at different times and different locations in their lives. Each of these friendships can be a best friend or forever friend in their lives at that time.

Just as Marsha, the theatre teacher, pointed out, she needs more than one friend.

There are individuals who will forge a solid relationship with the friend they are with at that moment in time. Other friendships can

180

be put on hold temporarily and picked up again at another point in time.

"I have four best friends in my life," remarks Sally, a fifty-year-old educator. "Only one of them lives in the city where I do now, the other three are elsewhere, but those relationships have lasted through lifetimes. Actually, those friends are best friends from different times in my life, but each of those relationships is strong enough to last forever."

Sally knows from experience that once the sixth level of friendship is reached, it becomes a lasting friendship. That person is a *forever* friend.

"The reason more people don't keep their friends for a lifetime is they don't trust and believe in the relationship," Sally continues. "With my friendships, I know if I went to Reno tomorrow, where one of my friends lives, she'd welcome me with open arms and we could pick up where we left off years ago. You see, I trust that relationship, I believe in it, even though I don't see that person anymore. And if there were any problems from our growth and change, I trust we'd work them out."

TRUST IN FRIENDSHIP

Indeed, no one can expect continuous and perfect harmony in any relationship. It is unrealistic to expect that in friendship.

"You must trust the friendship," agrees a twenty-three-year-old college student. "You must be able to fight and still care for each other. Nothing lasts unless you can fight and still love the other person. Enjoy each other's differences. When you can sit in the same room and just enjoy the other's presence, that's a friend. You don't have to talk—just enjoy the *thereness*, and it's O.K."

Nancy, a counselor, concurs. "You don't feel pressure to perform. You feel like you're not giving anything and you're getting so much. Those times are few and far between, but when they happen, you know you have a friendship. That friend will give you a kiss in the morning before you take a shower; give you a hug after you've played basketball and you're all sweaty—just because that friend knows you need it."

She goes on to say: "I think people like to be appreciated for their individuality. You treat a friend the way you want to be treated. We don't all have to like each other. Save it for the people who count. I'm so happy to have even one friend."

What we cherish most in our long-term friendships is the ability to be open and to enjoy the other person's openness with no judgment on either side.

You don't have to agree with your friend's opinions, simply accept them. Respect the person who lets you know how he really feels about something. Even if his feeling repulses you, respect him for his integrity. Don't judge his conclusion. Understand the risk he took in being honest with you and saying what he felt. He allowed you into his private world.

Tolerance is another key to long-term friendship. After all, tolerance and generosity become easier when an individual openly acknowledges his own failings.

A part of being human is making a mistake and admitting it. Remember the old advice: "Better to have tried and failed than never to have tried at all." We like to know that others have some of the same weaknesses we have.

Nevertheless, learn to give guidance and friendship when it's needed and learn when to ask for it yourself. Friends lend a sympathetic ear and offer constructive, supportive advice if they have it, and if they sense the other person is ready for it. At other times the sympathetic ear is enough. No advice is really needed. All that's needed is the presence of the other person.

So many people included in their depiction of a friend, "Someone who's there when I need him." But if you look at that statement closely, you realize it is impossible *all* the time. In reality, no one can be there *all* the time—every time you need him or her. That is too much to expect from any one human being.

However, what a friend can do is be there in spirit, in thoughts, in caring and sharing even if he can't be there in person.

Why do some friendships last forever? What's so special to you about an old friend? Here's how several people surveyed described their long-term friendships.

"There is a great element of trust with people I've known a long time. We level with each other. We share the same values even though some of those values have shifted, most have remained in our respective lives," offers a fifty-year-old newspaperman.

"I'm attracted to people with a special quality of humanity. When I see a friend after a long period of time, we pick up right where we left off. I'm always a little shocked and pleasantly surprised, when people reach out that warmly," says a stage designer named Craig, who travels a great deal.

182

"I don't expect friends to surprise me," declares a woman named Dorothy. "In fact, I'm surprised some of my old friends are still alive," she quips. "But what I mean is, I want them to be consistent. My old friends are the ones in similar situations to mine. We have things in common. I mean, whom are you going to be friends with—a rabbit? No—it's going to be someone you share interests with, someone you trust completely."

She paused for a moment. "Shared interests are so important, and I mean I'll share mine with you if you share yours with me. What really bugs me are the *takers*. Next to takers, I hate people who never say 'I'm sorry'!"

Dorothy's words suggest a good time to go back to Chapter 9, "How to Be a Friend," and look over the ten sentences for every friend to keep in his or her vocabulary.

A doctor in Philadelphia has a unique test for a friend of the "forever" type. "He's the one I'd name as the executor of my will. That's the best test I know for someone you would trust all the way. That friend I trust wholeheartedly, not only with what has been, but with what will be."

A well-known college administrator named Viola offers this: "My best friend is my sister. It's a lifelong friendship. She has the most marvelous point of view about human beings; she thinks everybody is wonderful. She is thoughtful and concerned and is interested in the world around her. She's not cynical or jaded—I can't stand cynics—she remembers everybody's birthday, anniversary, and special occasions—which I forget. She reads voraciously and always comes up with something new she's just discovered. She does nice little things for people all the time. She makes connections much more easily than I do. People tell her things. Everybody talks to her. She's amazing!"

Indeed, Viola's relationship with her sister is a unique and rare one.

WITHOUT FRIENDS

Friendship has meaning in everyone's life. Perhaps those who are without it—even temporarily—realize most vividly how important it really is.

For example, a therapist in a mental hospital ran an informal group for women from sixteen to sixty. This group met one evening a week. As this was a short-term hospital, and programs were voluntary, the members of the group changed frequently. They all, however, agreed that friendship was important to them. One of the primary concerns among most of these women was the lack of a friend, someone they could talk to, or call on for some kind of interaction.

Over the course of several months, the group created a list of qualities most desired in A FRIEND.

Here is the list (not necessarily in order of importance).

DESIRED QUALITIES IN A FRIEND

1. Loyalty
2. Honesty
3. Enjoys life
4. Serenity
5. Someone to talk to (confidentiality)
6. Sharing ideas, good and bad
7. Discretion
8. Cheerfulness
9. Sense of humor
10. Compassion or empathy

The one quality that shows up on this list and none other is serenity. Perhaps these women appreciate it more because they lack it.

Indeed, friendship or the absence of it has been a problem as long as man has been around or at least since recorded time.

In 1936, Dale Carnegie came out with a book, *How to Win Friends and Influence People,* which became a best seller. After nearly fifty years, that book is still going strong. That shows clearly how important friendship has been and still is to a great many people.

Indeed, friendship is humanity's greatest natural resource. Every person has the ability to use that natural resource to give his friendship and to receive the friendship of others. Our feelings, emotions, and spiritual essence are all a part of that great natural resource. Unlike our other natural resources, we do not deplete friendship by giving it freely. Like love, the more you give, the more you have to give. With the exchange of feelings and ideas we strengthen the bond of friendship.

In 1788, Robert Burns wrote four lines in praise of friendship that have come to be synonymous with the ritual welcome of the new year.

> Should auld acquaintance be forgot,
> And never brought to mind?
> Should auld acquaintance be forgot,
> And auld lang syne?

There has been such a concentration on *self* lately—*How to Be Your Own Best Friend, Self-Renewal, Looking Out for No. 1, Winning Through Intimidation*. It's time we got back to another basic need: interaction between self and another.

INTERACTIONS

Interaction is its own best reward. That interaction can see you through growth and change, shore you up when you need to be shored up, sympathize when you need sympathy, challenge you when you need a challenge. All of this is done through interaction. Through interaction, caring is acknowledged. There can be interaction in silence too.

All human beings need other human beings. Each of us needs to make contact with other people. Man by nature is a gregarious animal. He begins life as part of another person, then part of a family. From there he adds a variety of groups and individuals to enhance his sense of belonging.

"There should be more friendships in this world. There aren't enough friends, especially in the metropolitan area," comments a housewife from New York City named Betty.

"No man is an island, entire of itself." How many times have we heard that?

We all need others to relate to. In fact, the person who does not have a friendly ear to listen to him or her is the person who feels isolated. Why do so many people turn to professional counselors? Many times it's because nowhere in their own life do they have someone with that "sympathetic ear." What we need is more "we and us" and less "I-me-you."

Carson McCullers put it so beautifully in her play *A Member of the Wedding*, when the adolescent girl named Frankie said of her brother and his bride-to-be, "They are the *we* of me."

We all need the "WE of ME."

The desire for human contact is strong in all of us. That feeling cannot be ignored. It is vital to our well-being. That sense of connecting with other people is promoted by our interpersonal relationships. We learn from each other.

185

"I am a part of all that I have met." (Alfred, Lord Tennyson.)

One of the most important ways people grow and change is through friendship. Some people learn to think differently, view life in a different perspective, even transform their attitudes about life. Contact with a friend reaffirms the fact that you are a worthwhile human being. We function at our peak only when we know we are valued by other people. When no one cares, we don't care either. No one can live fully without friendship.

Not everyone achieves the sixth level of friendship or even the fifth. But everyone can function on one of the other levels. You cannot function all by yourself. It's impossible! It's dull!

"Nothing in the world is more interesting than people," affirms Viola, the college administrator.

LETDOWNS

What can you do when a friend lets you down? How do you equate the emotional reaction that occurs in the pit of your stomach with the long-term value of friendship? No friend deliberately sets out to hurt another, but sometimes the combination of circumstances conspires to bring about that result.

"Sometimes a friend will hit you with criticism at the worst possible time. That hurts. HURTS. And sometimes—you hurt back," exclaims Patty from Maryland. "What hurts me is when I'm overlooked. I mean—left out. I hate to be left out."

What we sometimes forget is that each individual is made up of many different qualities. For example, Tolstoy offered this thought-provoking insight:

> One of the most widespread superstitions is that every man has his own special definite qualities; that a man is kind, cruel, wise, stupid, energetic, apathetic, etc. Men are not like that. ... Men are like rivers; the water is the same in each, and alike in all; but every river is narrow here, is more rapid there, here slower, there broader, now clear, now cold, now dull, now warm. It is the same with men. Every man carries in himself the germs of every human quality, and sometimes one manifests itself, sometimes another, and the man often becomes unlike himself, while still remaining the same.

We are all made up of many parts. There are times when we feel at one with our universe and everything in it; other times when we feel like "the odd man out." Nothing goes right. Our friends turn in

186

another direction. Our expectations are not met. We are unhappy with ourselves and others.

Nevertheless, when things go wrong, don't dwell on them. Let your friend know you understand or you accept *him*—if not his action. Most of us don't plan to hurt those we care about, but it does happen in spite of our intentions. There are times when we let others down; our friends let us down.

A forty-year-old housewife in Connecticut says: "I just found myself asking: 'Is this all worth it? Is it worth all this fussing and talk?' My friend let me down *this* time, but that's the key. She let me down *this* time. She wasn't there when I needed her, she was needed someplace else. At least that was the decision she made. And that really hurt me. I felt pretty sorry for myself. After all, she's my best friend . . . and then I stopped to think about why she is my best friend. I thought about all the things she's done for me in the past; all the things we have brought to each other, the understanding, the compassion, the trust. Then I began to concentrate on the positives of my friend. I was still disappointed, yes. But I could honestly say, 'O.K., so she let me down this time, but remember all the other times' . . . and I made a list of her positives for myself. That way I could see how lucky I was to have her for a friend."

"My friend creates the opposite problem," admits Edmond from North Carolina. "He wants too much of me. If I am not careful, he becomes dependent on me. He's just been through a bad time, and I understand that. But friendship shouldn't be used for an unreasonable state of dependency. Friendship shouldn't be abused."

"There can be a kind of draining in a friendship," explains Marilyn, a psychologist in Pennsylvania. "When neither person brings anything new to the relationship, it must constantly feed off of what is already there. It's almost an incestuous friendship. There is too much dependence on what's already been discovered. Friends shouldn't get too intimate. Some skeletons are better left in the closet."

She thought for a moment and then added: "Times when I feel let down are times when my friend won't accept what I'm willing to give but wants more. There is a part of myself which is very private. I'm not willing to share that with anybody. Any friend of mine must respect that part of me or I can't have that person for a friend."

Unlike Marilyn, some people need to share their intimate feelings with others.

A thirty-year-old bartender from Queens, New York, talks about the many people who use him for the friend they wish they had. He says: "The man without a friend will tell me the most intimate things—things he probably wouldn't tell his own doctor. I don't mind listening, but I always feel kind of sorry for the guy, because I know if he has to talk to a stranger—the bartender—he probably doesn't have anyone else who will listen."

Another perceptive listener asks: "Why do some people find it so difficult to reach out and say, 'I need you,' to a friend? They have no trouble saying, 'I'm hungry' or 'I'm thirsty.' Those are physical needs. Emotional needs are just as important."

Remember, friends aren't mind readers. Even a sensitive friend is not clairvoyant. No one can be completely tuned into your needs at this particular moment in time. Sometimes you have to say it. I NEED . . . Tell your friend: "I need some quiet time. Could you come back later?"

MEANINGS

What does friendship mean to you? Although everyone needs it, it is of greater importance in some people's lives than it is in others.

"I really like people. I like all kinds of people. And I'm confident enough in my own desirability as a friend that if I have to make the contact seven or eight times out of ten, I will. As long as the other person does reciprocate the other two or three times," says a thirty-five-year-old woman from Ohio.

A forty-year-old salesman named Jim says this: "What does friendship mean to me? It means a lot. It's like faith. Friends are able to share an activity; theatre, baseball, church, etc. It's a bonding. Sharing one of the creative arts helps create that bond for me."

Jim continues: "The *bond* is a mutual trust and caring feeling. The emotional part has to be there. Friendship is like *faith*—which is more emotional than intellectual."

Six college students from the same New York school offer their views on what friendship means in their lives:

A young woman says: "Friendship means more to me than almost anything else in my life. I try to see the good qualities in my friends, even when they don't know they have them. I believe in them not only for what they are but for what they can be."

Another offers this: "A friend for me is someone who will help in times of need; someone who will try to save me from pain without distorting the truth."

188

Still another says: "With a friend there is a comfortable ease. You no longer need to do things to please. You just spend time together, just enjoy the other person's company. You can talk honestly about almost anything no matter how personal and know the friend will be understanding. They won't use that knowledge against you."

"When you care a lot for someone," adds another, "you don't have to go to her church or her club or her—anything. You don't have to be just like her. She liked you, or was attracted to you—as the person you are. My friend is someone who understands and cares and knows how *present* to be. Some people intrude on your life. A real friend doesn't. She's just there when you want her to be but knows when you don't want her around."

A young actress from Brooklyn explains what friendship means in her life: "A friend is someone who's there when I need her, if not physically; then spiritually. That someone is always honest with me even though she may risk hurting me. And I must be able to say, 'STOP! You're hurting me.' And she will stop. No one is perfect. We work through our problems with love and patience. Friendship is a fragile thing."

Ronald from St. Louis says: "Friendship is very important to me. My friends are all *best* friends, best in some way; best at some time. I'd go to any length for my friends and I feel they would go to any length for me. We reciprocate not because we have to, but because we want to."

CHANGING NEEDS

There are many different levels of friendship. Remember the *Six Levels of Friendship* described in Chapter 4. Different people have different requirements. The same person can have friendships on totally different levels. Friendship needs change at different stages in our lives. Just as we change and grow so do others. The ability to accept the changes in others as well as ourselves is an important element in holding on to our friends. It is only the person who is afraid to change who doesn't grow. That is a critical part of accepting another person; the ability to accept the changes in that person.

"Friendship shouldn't be exploited or taken advantage of," a sales manager comments, "nor should it be bartered. You don't owe me a favor just because I did one for you. Favors are freely given without thought of return. Otherwise, it's not a favor."

To summarize, some people have the ability and desire to have a good friend close by wherever they are in life. As they grow and change, move from one part of the country to another, they still maintain the old friendships as well as the new. They keep their long-term friendships. And then they work to create another close friend where they are at the present time.

Other people prefer to have several friends on the less personal level. Still others are satisfied with having people on the good neighbor level. Whichever you prefer, or need at the time, one fact is obvious: everyone needs somebody. We all need friends and need a connection with another human being. We need to take an interest in another person's well-being and contribute to that person's comfort and progress.

Sir Edwin Arnold offers these thoughts on the subject in his poem "Destiny":

> Somewhere there waiteth in this world of ours
>   For one lone soul, another lonely soul—
> Each chasing each through all the weary hours,
>   And meeting strangely at one sudden goal;
> Then blend they—like green leaves with golden flowers,
>   Into one beautiful and perfect whole—
> And life's long night is ended, and the way
> Lies open onward to eternal day.

Remember the advice from Samuel Johnson:

> If a man does not make new acquaintances as he advances through life, he will soon find himself left alone. A man, sir, should keep his friendship in constant repair.

Friendship should be described as "the working relationship."

We all desire friendship, even those of us who don't have it. First, there must be an environment of safety and support for friendship to grow. There must be a comfortable, relaxed atmosphere. A level of honesty and trust must be present. There is no room for competition in friendship. We must accept others' limitations as we expect them to accept ours. The friendship bond is special and unique. It is open-ended because it continues to grow and change.

There are no shortcuts to friendship, no magic wand to tap and make friendship come true. It is a working relationship, a continual process that necessitates continual nurture. Remember, always give a friend the benefit of the doubt.

190

Recall the little boy's wish at the wishing well: "Please make me be the kind of person I'd like to have for a friend."

If there is a golden rule for friendship, it is this:

BE THE FRIEND YOU'D LIKE TO HAVE.

Follow that advice, and you'll have friends in your life. We all need reminders to keep our friendships "in constant repair."

To be the friend you'd like to have, here are ten suggestions to remember and practice as often as you can:

TEN COMMANDMENTS FOR FRIENDSHIP

Forgive a friend.
Respect a friend.
Inspire him to do his best.
Enjoy his company.
Nurture the relationship.
Don't compete.
Support a friend.
Honor a friend with honesty.
Ignore his faults.
Provide comfort when he's down and joy when he's up.

P. S.

"Without friendship life is nothing."
A Latin proverb

With friendship
life is everything it should be.
P. S.